Sovereign Men
Self-Rule for Middle-Aged Men
When the Rules Keep Changing

By Dr. Dell Gines

Copyright © 2026 by Dell Gines

All rights reserved. No part of this book may be reproduced, distributed, or transmitted in any form or by any means, including photocopying, recording, or other electronic or mechanical methods, without the prior written permission of the copyright owner, except in the case of brief quotations embodied in critical reviews and certain other noncommercial uses permitted by copyright law.

ISBN: 979-8-9943651-0-6

Table of Contents

Why this Book Matters...4

Chapter 1 - The Middle-Aged Man..................12

Chapter 2 - The Response 20

Chapter 3 - The Philosophy 32

Chapter 4 - The Science 48

Chapter 5 - The Center 58

Chapter 6 - The Purpose......................................70

Chapter 7 - The Adaptability..............................84

Chapter 8 - The Authority 94

Chapter 9 - The Sovereign State.....................108

Glossary..116

Appendix..122

About the Author 141

Why this Book Matters

You reach your front door after work but pause. The knob is in your hand, yet you hesitate. The house is right there, full of people you love, but something tugs inside. You handled every task today, solved problems, and even cracked a joke in a meeting. Still, in this quiet moment, you feel hollow. That pause signals a bigger truth. Many middle-aged men feel it but rarely name it.

Who This Book Is For

This book is written for middle-aged men. Not because younger or older men cannot benefit. Because this is where the pressure concentrates.

You have lived long enough to build something. A career. A family. A reputation. You have also lived long enough to feel the cracks. The body that used to bounce back now sends invoices. The title that once felt solid now feels like a target. The relationships that used to run on autopilot now require attention you do not have. The rules you followed to get here no longer apply, and no one handed you a new playbook.

This is the age when roles shift faster than identity can follow. Kids leave home. Parents need care. Careers plateau or vanish. The future that once stretched out endlessly now has a visible end. Men in their twenties and thirties can outrun this pressure for a while. Men past sixty-five have often made peace with it or collapsed under it. Men in the middle are still in the fight, and the fight is real.

If you are in that window, this book is for you.

The Modern State of Middle-Aged Men

Here is what the data shows. It is not pretty.

More than half of American men report that no one really knows them. Not fully. Not deeply. They move through rooms full of people and still feel unseen. They have colleagues, not confidants. They have responsibilities, not relationships. When a man feels unknown, the risk of despair multiplies. Men who feel invisible are more than twice as likely to consider ending their lives.

The isolation runs deeper than loneliness. It touches identity itself. Modern life rewards production and role-playing. You become the go-to employee, the steady partner, the on-call dad. Those roles matter, yet over time they can swallow the person inside. Many men still define manhood as being a provider. That definition carries weight in a shaky economy. When bills pile up or careers stall, the man who cannot provide faces a devastating reckoning. Men who fail to meet the provider standard are sixteen times more likely to contemplate suicide.

The mirrors that once reflected your worth start to crack. You retire from sports. You switch jobs or lose one. Your kids leave home. The labels that felt solid, provider, leader, fixer, shift or disappear. Psychologists call this **meta-loss**. It is the slow erosion of identity when the external markers vanish and nothing internal remains.

Friendships fade at the same time. Many men tie friendship to shared action. A weekly basketball run, lunch at the office, a project in the garage. Midlife shifts schedules. Children, divorce, or relocation cut those ties. Living alone can sharpen isolation, but living with family does not erase it. A man can sit at dinner and still feel unseen if he thinks he must handle every problem on his own.

Then the body speaks up. Knees ache after simple tasks. Energy dips before the day ends. The scale creeps higher. These signs remind a man of time passing fast. Popular jokes about the midlife crisis hide a harder truth: the gap between what life demands and what the body now gives. When strength wanes just as duties remain heavy, frustration grows.

Add to this the noise. Online spaces promise answers but deliver warped communities built on anger and competition. Traditional masculine codes tighten their grip even as the world asks for something different. The rules contradict. Be tough. Be open. Be strong. Be vulnerable. Be a leader. Share the load. The confusion is real, and the cost shows up in families, workplaces, and the mirror.

Five Pressures at Once

Notice how these forces blend. Picture a pot on the stove with five burners. Each pressure is one flame set to low.

Hidden mental pain that wears a straight face. Rigid masculine rules that tighten instead of guide. Shaky work realities that shift the ground. Shrinking friendship circles that leave you alone in a crowd. And a body in slow decline that reminds you of limits.

Alone, each only warms the water. Together, they push it to boil. A sharp comment at work might trigger deep rage because it lands on top of chronic pain and money fear. A sudden retreat into video games could mix social drift with shame about weight gain. Treating one pressure without naming the others keeps the pot simmering.

This is the modern state of middle-aged men. Not weakness. Not moral failure. Pressure that hits from five directions at once while the old tools no longer work.

Why Sovereignty Matters

This book starts with that pause. The core point is simple: a man needs to rule himself. Not perform for others. Not react to pressure. Not fade into the background. Rule himself. This book offers a philosophy built on that claim. We call it the **Sovereign State**.

Why sovereign? The word carries weight. A sovereign nation answers to no foreign power. It sets its own laws. It governs its own territory. A sovereign man does the same thing, but the territory is internal. He governs his own thoughts, emotions, and actions. Not the scoreboard. Not the role he plays. Not the critics. He is the rightful authority over his own responses, his own choices, his own way of being.

This matters because most men have surrendered that authority. Not in one dramatic moment, but in a slow slide. They gave the scoreboard power to decide their worth. They gave the role power to dictate their moves. They gave the critics power to define what they could become. Each surrender felt like safety at the time. Each surrender left them with less ground to stand on.

Sovereignty is the claim that you can take it back. Not perfectly. Not without struggle. But the claim matters. It says the throne belongs to you, even when pressure tries to push you off it. It says your responses are yours to choose, even when old habits pull hard. It says your identity does not depend on titles, status, or applause.

The Sovereign State is a philosophy of self-rule. Center is the mechanism that makes self-rule possible. When body, mind, and emotion align, you can actually govern yourself instead of just wishing you could. Center is where sovereignty becomes real, where the claim meets the capacity to act on it.

Why This Framework Is Different

You have seen other approaches to masculinity. The internet is full of them. Strong man. Stoic man. Dominant man. Provider. Warrior. Alpha. Most of these frameworks start with an identity ideal, then prescribe behaviors meant to approximate that ideal. They tell you what to be. The Sovereign State does something else. It teaches you how to stay governed while moving toward something that matters.

That difference is structural, not cosmetic.

Most masculinity systems treat calm and discipline as character traits you either have or lack. This framework treats them as states you actively produce and restore. Centering is infrastructure, not a personality test. Your body reacts faster than your thoughts. Before you can reason through a situation, your nervous system has already set the terms. If you want to govern yourself under pressure, you have to work with the body, not just the mind. This is not philosophy alone. It is mechanism.

Most masculinity systems collapse identity into outward behavior. Assertiveness. Leadership. Stoicism. Dominance. They measure the man by his performance. This framework separates governance from performance. Self-rule comes first. The ability to remain centered, adaptive, and directed under pressure is the foundation. Performance emerges downstream, shaped by purpose rather than applause. You do not perform your way into sovereignty. You govern yourself, and clean action follows.

Most masculinity systems lean hard in one direction. Either cognitive mastery, meaning mindset and discipline and mental toughness. Or primal embodiment, meaning instinct and aggression and raw physicality. This framework treats both as levers. Your nervous system and your cognition work together. A thought can trigger a physical response. A physical state can shape what you think and feel. They form a loop. Sovereignty requires access to both directions, chosen based on what the moment actually needs rather than what an ideology demands.

Most masculinity systems promise certainty, belonging, or moral clarity. They sell reassurance. This framework is indifferent to reassurance. Purpose is not about feeling right. It is about maintaining direction despite uncertainty, imperfection, or discomfort. Purpose over perfection. You do not wait for ideal conditions. You move now with what you have.

Most masculinity systems reward rigidity. Hold frame. Never bend. Never show uncertainty. This framework treats adaptability as strength because it preserves agency across changing environments. Center travels with the man. It is not dependent on dominance, approval, or control. You can enter different rooms, face different pressures, absorb different errors, and still keep moving because your foundation is internal.

Finally, this framework avoids the most common trap. Masculinity as compensation. Many approaches try to fix insecurity by amplifying traits. Louder. Harder. More dominant. More stoic. The Sovereign State does not amplify. It stabilizes. When the system is stable, traits express cleanly or not at all, depending on what purpose requires. You are not proving anything. You are governing something.

In short, most masculinity philosophies tell men what to be. This one teaches men how to stay governed while moving toward something that matters.

The Sovereign State: A Different Way

Imagine the final quarter of a football game. The coach gathers the team, wipes the whiteboard clean, and says, "Forget the noise. Let's play our game." The Sovereign State is that sideline moment lived every day. It is the choice to return to center before the next play. No crowd can rattle it. No scoreboard can define it.

This is not a new religion or a guru ritual. It is a practical framework grounded in how nervous systems work, how emotions regulate, and how bodies and minds align under pressure. When your body calms, your prefrontal cortex engages. Vision widens. Choices clarify. In plain terms, stillness sharpens the mind.

The Sovereign State offers an internal anchor that holds when external markers shift. It does not depend on your title, your income, or your physical peak. It does not require perfect conditions or perfect performance. It asks for one thing: that you choose to act from center rather than react from fear, numbness, or retreat.

What This Book Offers

This book provides a framework for middle-aged men. It defines a way of being, not a list of tasks. You will not find step-by-step instructions or daily drills. You will find a philosophy that creates identity. It names what the Sovereign State is, what it is not, and why it matters for men caught between outdated scripts and modern confusion.

The language stays plain. The examples stay real. The goal is clarity, not cleverness. This is peer-to-peer conversation between grown men who know life is messy and are done pretending otherwise.

The Path Forward

The world will keep pulling. Roles will keep shifting. Economic pressure will continue. Cultural arguments will not resolve cleanly. You cannot stop that tide. You can, however, anchor yourself.

The Sovereign State is not about arriving at perfection. It is about moving from center in imperfect conditions. Purpose over perfection. Adaptation without breaking. Same man, every room. These are not slogans. This is self-governance in a complex world.

Frameworks can change your life. Not because the words are magic, but because they name what you already sense. That pause at the door is not confusion. It is a signal. Something inside you knows the old paths are not working. This book offers a different path. One that lets you stay present in your own life while the world moves around you.

That pause at the door is real. It is not weakness. It is a signal that something inside you already knows. This book names what you sense and gives it structure.

The pause brought you here. The next pages show you what to do with it.

Chapter 1

The Middle-Aged Man

You catch yourself in the bathroom mirror before the day starts. The face looking back is familiar but not quite right. More gray. More lines. Eyes that look tired even after sleep. You stand there a moment longer than usual, not fixing your hair or checking your teeth, just looking. Something in that reflection doesn't match how you feel inside. The man in the mirror is older than the man you think you are.

You shake it off and start the day. But that pause stays with you. It marks a wider turbulence many men face at middle age.

Five pressures now hit middle-aged men at the same time: hidden mental pain, rigid masculine rules, shaky work realities, shrinking friendship circles, and the body's slow decline. Each pressure alone can strain a person. Together they form a weight that leaves many men drifting, angry, or numb. Before we can talk about steadier ground, we map the assault.

Hidden Mental Pain

Mental pain often hides behind a straight face. Men report depression less often than women, yet suicide data tells a different story. The highest rates tend to show up among men in their forties and fifties. The gap between what men feel and what they report is vast.

You know the pattern. A man jokes at work and cries in the shower at night. He answers "I'm fine" so many times the words lose meaning. He watches his mood sink but calls it stress, calls it the job, calls it anything except what it is. His wife notices something is off and asks. He says it's nothing. She asks again a week later. He changes the subject. The distance grows.

Silence thickens because the old script says men handle their own weight. Asking for help feels like failure. Admitting you're struggling feels like burdening people who already depend on you. So the pain stays hidden, and hidden pain grows roots. It shows up as irritability, as withdrawal, as a shorter fuse with the kids, as a drink that becomes three drinks that becomes every night.

The medical system often misses it. Men describe their symptoms differently. They talk about being tired, being stressed, having trouble focusing. They don't use the clinical words that trigger a diagnosis. Doctors hear "I'm worn out" and prescribe rest instead of recognizing what's underneath. The pain stays untreated because it never gets named.

Rigid Masculine Rules

From childhood most boys hear the same rules. Be strong. Fix problems. Provide. Don't complain. Handle it. Those ideas once gave clear direction, but they turn into iron bars when life shifts.

Lose a job and the old script says you failed. Struggle to cover bills and shame floods in before reason can speak. The rule "never show weakness" blocks honest talk with the people closest to you. Your wife asks what's wrong and you say "nothing" because admitting the truth feels like handing her a broken man.

Your kids sense something is off but you won't burden them. Pressure builds behind a locked door because the rules say that's where it belongs.

The rules also contradict now. Be tough, but also be open. Be strong, but also be vulnerable. Lead the family, but also share the load equally. One voice says traditional masculinity is the answer. Another says it's the problem. You try to follow the rules and find they point in opposite directions. So you freeze, or you pick one and get criticized for ignoring the other.

The men who raised you probably followed a simpler code. Work hard, provide, stay steady, don't talk about feelings. That code came with costs they never mentioned, but at least it was clear. Now the clarity is gone. The expectations multiply and conflict. You're supposed to be the rock and also be emotionally available. You're supposed to lead and also defer. You're supposed to embody traditional strength and also reject traditional patterns. No one can be all of these things at once, but the criticism comes no matter which version you choose.

Shaky Work Realities

Work used to offer a stable identity. Show up, do the job, retire with a pension and a handshake. That world is gone.

Automation eats roles that existed for decades. Mergers delete departments overnight. Younger workers cost less and know the new tools cold. A man raised on the promise of loyalty exchanged for security watches that promise break. The company you gave fifteen years restructures, and your title disappears into a role that reports to someone ten years younger.

A layoff at fifty lands harder than a layoff at twenty-five. College tuition, mortgage payments, aging parents. The bills do not pause because your income did. Even men who keep their jobs feel the floor wobble. Performance reviews measure things that didn't exist five years ago. The rules change, and the target moves, and tomorrow feels less certain than it did yesterday.

Shrinking Friendship Circles

Many men tie friendship to shared action. A weekly basketball run, lunch with coworkers, a project in the garage with a buddy. Midlife shifts schedules and scatters the people you used to see.

The guys you grabbed a beer with moved away, got divorced, or just stopped calling. Your work friends belonged to the last job, and the new office hasn't produced anyone you'd trust with real talk. The garage project ended. The basketball knees gave out. The hunting trip that used to happen every fall quietly dropped off the calendar three years ago and nobody mentioned it.

Men's social circles tend to shrink in middle age. The pattern is common enough that most men recognize it even if they've never seen the research. Living alone sharpens isolation, but living with family does not erase it. A man can sit at dinner surrounded by people who love him and still feel unseen. Not because they don't care. Because he's convinced himself he has to handle everything alone, and that wall keeps even the closest people on the other side.

The loneliness is hard to name because it doesn't look like loneliness. You're not sitting alone in a dark apartment. You're at the kid's soccer game, at the company happy hour, at the neighborhood cookout. But surface contact is not the same as being known. When something heavy lands, you realize there's no one to call. No one who would get it. The circle shrank so slowly you didn't notice until you needed it and found it gone.

The Body's Slow Decline

Then the body speaks up. Knees ache after a simple yard task. Energy dips before the afternoon ends. The scale creeps higher. Recovery from a workout takes days instead of hours. Sleep gets lighter and shorter. Something always hurts now.

You used to play through pain. Now you manage around it. The shoulder that was fine last year now wakes you up at night if you sleep on it wrong. The back that handled anything now seizes up when you bend to tie your shoes. You adjust. You stop doing the things that hurt. And then one day you realize how much you've stopped doing.

These signs remind a man that time runs in one direction. The gap between what life demands and what the body delivers grows wider each year. You still carry the same responsibilities, maybe more, but the machine underneath is wearing down. Your father probably went through the same thing, but he never talked about it. Neither do you.

Popular jokes about the "midlife crisis" hide a harder truth. This is not about buying a sports car. It is about watching your physical capacity decline while the demands stay constant or rise. Strength fades at the exact moment you are supposed to be holding everything together. The young guys at work have energy you remember having. Now you budget yours like a limited resource.

The Stack Effect

Picture a pot on the stove with five burners underneath. Each pressure is one flame set to low. Alone, each flame only warms the water. Together, they push it to a boil.

A sharp comment at work might trigger deep rage because it lands on top of chronic pain, money fear, and a shrinking circle of friends who would understand. A retreat into screens for hours might look like laziness but could be the only break from a body that hurts and a role that feels like a trap. Treating one pressure without naming the others keeps the pot simmering.

This is not about one bad quarter or a rough patch that will pass. The pressures are structural. They arrive together and reinforce each other. The man who loses his job also loses the coworkers who were his main social contact. The man whose body declines also loses the pickup games that gave him an outlet. Each pressure makes the others worse.

Meta-Loss

Under this stack, something deeper happens.

The markers that once told you who you were start to fail. The provider identity cracks when income feels uncertain. The protector identity fades when the body slows. The leader identity blurs when the rules keep changing and every choice gets second-guessed by someone.

This is meta-loss. It is not one crisis. It is the erosion of the structure you used to stand on.

You built a self out of roles and achievements. Father. Husband. Professional. Athlete. Provider. Those labels felt solid. They told you what kind of man you were. They gave you a place in the world and a script for how to act. Now the labels shift or disappear. The kids leave and the father role changes shape. The career stalls and the professional title feels hollow. The body gives out and the athlete is gone. The income wobbles and the provider identity cracks.

Each single loss is manageable. Men handle loss. That's what we do. But meta-loss is different. It is not losing something you have. It is losing the structure that tells you who you are. It is waking up one day and realizing the version of yourself you spent decades building no longer fits the life you're living.

The question stops being "how do I fix this problem" and becomes "who am I now that the old markers are gone?" That question has no easy answer. And most men were never taught how to ask it.

The Reach

Meta-loss does not make men weak. It makes them reach.

When the ground shifts, you grab for anything solid. Some reach for dominance, hoping control will bring stability. Some reach for performance, hoping the right moves will earn safety. Some reach for invisibility, hoping to avoid the criticism by disappearing.

Each is an attempt to find solid ground. Each is understandable. And each ends in surrender. Handing control to something outside yourself.

The next chapter maps those three responses in detail. You will see how each one starts as protection and ends as a trap. You will recognize patterns you've seen in other men, and maybe patterns you've seen in yourself.

That moment in the mirror is not vanity. It is a signal. Something is pressing, and the old answers are not working.

THE FIVE PRESSURES OF MIDDLE AGE

HIDDEN MENTAL PAIN
Emotional struggles are often concealed, leading to isolation and untreated distress.

RIGID MASCULINE RULES
Outdated social expectations create internal conflict and block honest communication.

SHAKY WORK REALITIES
The traditional promise of a stable career has been replaced by professional uncertainty.

SHRINKING FRIENDSHIPS
Social circles often contract, leading to a profound sense of **loneliness**.

THE BODY'S DECLINE
Physical capacity wanes just as **life's responsibilities** and demands peak.

Chapter 2

The Response

You scroll through three short clips on your phone. The first shows a man pounding iron in a garage gym, barking that real men "take back power" and stop apologizing. The second follows a guy in a nice suit who hits every deadline, gets the promotion, and admits in a podcast interview that he feels nothing anymore. The third features a soft-spoken man who shrugs through a conversation, agreeing with everything, offering nothing, fading into the background of his own life.

Three different men. Three different styles. You might admire one, pity another, and dismiss the third. But look closer. Each one is responding to the same pressure. Each one is trying to solve the same problem. And each one has handed control to something outside himself.

The Causal Frame

When rules change and the old scripts fail, men reach for something. The reach is not a character flaw. It is an adaptive response to confusion.

Some reach for dominance, hoping control will bring stability. Some numb out, hoping performance will earn safety. Some erase themselves, hoping invisibility will stop the criticism. Each response is understandable. Each one starts as protection. None provides foundation.

All three are reactions to pressure. All three hand the throne to something outside. The scoreboard. The role. The critics. In each case, the man stops governing himself and starts being governed.

As you read the three paths below, test yourself with honest questions. When life stings, do I swing back harder? Do I keep the show running but feel empty behind the smile? Do I soften so much that I barely leave a footprint? Your honest answer marks where you stand.

The Red Pill Path

Mark's alarm goes off at 4:45 AM. He doesn't hit snooze. At 54, he moves with coiled intensity. The morning is a sequence: cold plunge, raw eggs, a heavy lifting session in the garage gym where he logs every pound and every rep. He tracks his macros, his sleep score, his testosterone levels. He sees life as a marketplace and refuses to be undervalued.

At the office, he sizes up every room. Who's the threat. Who's the asset. Who can be dismissed. He scoffs at colleagues who let themselves go, calling them "betas" under his breath. He reads forums that rank men by status and women by desirability. The language is clinical. The worldview is competitive. Every interaction is a test.

At dinner, his daughter talks about her day, but Mark is half-listening, scrolling through his phone, tracking investment tips from a guy who calls himself an alpha. His wife asks him a question and he answers with a clipped, authoritative tone. He wins the exchange. He always wins the exchange. But later that night, staring at the ceiling, he feels a familiar gnawing loneliness. He has a perfect record, but the stadium is empty.

The Red Pill path promises a return to power. It says: the world has rules, and if you learn them, you can win. It offers a clear chart of winners and losers. Status, strength, dominance. These are the metrics. Hit them and you matter. Miss them and you don't.

The promise hits hard because the weight feels real. Bills stack up, hairlines thin, and the rules at home and work keep changing. The Red Pill claims to explain it all in one shot. Women chase alpha traits. Society rewards strength. You've been lied to about what masculinity means, and now here's the truth.

On the surface the plan sounds useful. Lift heavier. Track your numbers. Dress sharper. Speak with authority. Each step can improve health or confidence. But the toolbox hides a trap. Every gain serves a scoreboard, not your own direction. You add five pounds to the bench press but feel flat if someone else adds ten. You land a raise but feel poor when a stranger online posts a bigger one. The goalposts slide. You sprint harder without ever crossing the finish line.

The Red Pill also narrows how you see people. Women become hunters of status, always testing, always trading. Men become rivals or tools. When you view everyone that way, warmth cools. Trust fades because you assume hidden motives. Friendly conversations become competitions. Even good moments feel like temporary truces before the next battle.

Relationships burn under this heat. A wife who once felt like a partner now feels like an opponent to be managed. Friends who don't share the worldview become liabilities. The circle shrinks to people who validate the scoreboard. And the scoreboard is never satisfied.

This is self-rule surrendered to the scoreboard. The numbers decide your worth. External validation rules. You look like you're in control, but the control runs on fear. Fear of falling behind. Fear of being seen as weak. Fear of losing rank. The grip never loosens because the threat never ends.

The Hollow State

David is the model of reliability. At the office, his projects come in on time and under budget. His email response time is legendary. His desk is clean, his calendar is full, and his performance reviews are spotless. He is praised for his steadiness. A rock for his company and his family.

But inside, there is nothing.

He sits in meetings, nodding and taking perfect notes, while his mind feels like a blank screen. He watches his son's soccer game and cheers at the right moments, but the joy doesn't reach his chest. He tells his wife he loves her, and he does, but the words come out flat, like lines he's memorized. He goes through the day executing tasks with precision while some essential part of him watches from a distance, uninvolved.

David can't remember the last time he wanted something for himself. Not performed enthusiasm because others expected it. Actually wanted something. His own desires have faded so far into the background that he's not sure they exist anymore.

The Hollow State shows up when a man stays in motion yet feels absent from his own life. He meets every duty but invests nothing of himself. The causes stack up over time.

First is shifting social ground. The markers of manhood that once felt solid now face daily debate. Traditional roles get labeled as outdated or harmful. A fifty-year-old who built his identity on being a provider and protector watches those roles get criticized in think pieces and social media posts. He's not sure what "good man" means anymore. So he keeps working, keeps producing, and wades through doubt. Motion stays. Meaning slips.

Second is work fatigue. Jobs that once felt stable now change constantly. Mergers, layoffs, new metrics, new platforms. The target moves every quarter. You may still clock in but wonder if your role matters. Your best effort feels like running a treadmill that speeds up without warning. Fighting the machine seems pointless, so you keep pace on autopilot. You get through tasks, then shut down the minute you leave.

Third is silent protest. Part of you senses the rules keep changing faster than you can adjust. Rather than risk a misstep, you choose quiet compliance. Stay neutral. Say less. Give only what is required. It feels safe, but the cost is high. Over time your own desires fade from view. Life becomes a to-do list, not a story you want to tell.

Living hollow brings hidden harm. The man who feels nothing is not at peace. He's numb. The numbness protects him from the confusion and criticism, but it also cuts him off from joy, from desire, from the sense that his life is his own. He can run the schedule but cannot remember why any of it matters.

This is self-rule surrendered to the role. The expectation decides your moves. The throne sits empty while the body keeps working. You show up, you deliver, you perform. But the man inside has checked out. And the longer he's gone, the harder it is to find him again.

The Void

Steve's wife is talking about their son's slipping grades, her voice tight with worry. Part of Steve wants to set a firm line. Clear expectations, real consequences, the kind of structure his own father would have enforced without hesitation. But then another voice cuts in, one he's absorbed from years of articles and podcasts warning against authoritarian parenting, against toxic patterns, against being the wrong kind of man.

He immediately shrinks.

"You're probably right," he says, interrupting his own half-formed thought. "We should just give him space to figure it out. The last thing I want is to be controlling."

His wife's shoulders slump. She wasn't looking for a dictator. She was looking for a partner. But Steve has already disappeared. In his effort to avoid being the wrong kind of man, he has stopped being any kind of man at all. He has made himself so small that there's nothing left to hold onto.

The Void appears when a man erases parts of himself to avoid judgment. Unsure which version of masculinity will be accepted, he chooses silence. The move feels safe at first. Over time it drains everything.

Three currents pull him there. First, constant critique of traditional masculinity. Some of that critique has merit. Old patterns caused real harm. But when every masculine trait faces suspicion, a man starts to doubt his own instincts. Firm resolve becomes potential aggression. Protecting your family becomes controlling behavior. Speaking directly becomes dominating the conversation. Rather than navigate which critiques have merit and which don't, he trims everything that might draw fire. He tells fewer stories, shares fewer opinions, makes himself smaller so no one can call him out.

Second, shaky work. Steady income once marked success. Now layoffs and age bias cut deep. When a man's professional identity collapses at fifty, rebuilding feels risky. The less he tries, the less he can fail. But retreat blocks the new wins that could restore self-trust. He stops reaching for anything because reaching means risking, and he's tired of losing.

Third, mixed models of manhood. One article cheers open vulnerability. The next podcast pushes raw assertiveness. Social media cycles through contradictory advice faster than anyone can follow. What earns praise today draws criticism tomorrow. Unsure what version of himself will be accepted, the safest plan is no plan. He stays neutral, hopes to offend no one, and blends into the background.

Life in the Void hurts in quiet ways. The man who fades doesn't explode or collapse. He just becomes less. His opinions disappear from family discussions. His voice gets softer in meetings until people stop asking what he thinks. His wife stops expecting him to weigh in on decisions because he never does. His kids learn that Dad will go along with whatever everyone else wants.

The Void sells safety through erasure. But erasure is not peace. It is slow disappearance. The man trades his presence for the absence of criticism, and the trade hollows him out.

This is self-rule given up entirely. The critics decide, so the man steps down rather than risk ruling badly. He no longer sits on the throne. He has walked away from it. And with each step back, he loses more of himself.

The Common Thread

Three paths. Three different styles. One shared failure.

The Red Pill man looks aggressive. The Hollow man looks competent. The Void man looks agreeable. But underneath, they share the same orientation. All three are reacting. All three have handed control to something outside themselves.

The Red Pill reacts to status threats. Every move is calibrated to the scoreboard. Rise in rank and you feel good. Slip in rank and you feel worthless. The scoreboard governs.

The Hollow State reacts to expectations. Every move is calibrated to what others want. Meet the expectation and you're safe. Miss it and you're exposed. The role governs.

The Void reacts to criticism. Every move is calibrated to avoid judgment. Stay invisible and you're safe. Be seen and you're a target. The critics govern.

In each case, the environment is governing the man. He is being moved rather than choosing movement.

This is the core problem. Not the specific path. The orientation itself. When you live in reaction, life becomes a loop. Stimulus, response. Stimulus, response. You never set the agenda. You only respond to agendas set by others. You are governed, not governing.

The man on the Red Pill thinks he's taking control. But he's a slave to the scoreboard. The man in the Hollow State thinks he's being responsible. But he's a slave to the expectations. The man in the Void thinks he's being safe. But he's a slave to the critics. None of them is free. None of them is steering. They are all passengers in their own lives, reacting to whatever comes through the window.

The Sovereign Way

You have now seen three mirrors. The first showed a clenched fist, always measuring, always competing, always afraid of falling behind. The second showed a blank face, executing tasks with precision while the person inside watches from far away. The third showed a faint outline, fading into the background to avoid being seen at all.

If you saw yourself in any of those mirrors, you are not alone. Most men lean toward one of these paths when pressure builds. The lean makes sense. The path offers something. Dominance offers the feeling of control. Performance offers the feeling of safety. Invisibility offers the feeling of peace. But each feeling is borrowed. And each path eventually presents the bill.

So what is left?

There is a fourth way. It is not about winning every contest, drifting through tasks, or shrinking out of sight. It is about governing yourself. Choosing your responses instead of reacting. Moving from the inside out instead of being pushed from the outside in.

We call this the Sovereign State. Sovereign means self-ruling. Not ruled by the scoreboard. Not ruled by expectations. Not ruled by critics. Ruled by your own intention, your own values, your own chosen direction.

The Sovereign State does not ask you to become someone else. It does not hand you a rigid ideal to chase. It offers something different: a way to stay steady when the ground shifts. A way to adapt without losing yourself. A way to be the same man in every room while adjusting to what each room actually requires.

The next chapter unpacks how that works. You will see the philosophy underneath it, the structure that makes it possible, and why it holds when the other three paths break. The diagnosis is complete. Now we build.

Visit Appendix C for Path Reflection

RED PILL, HOLLOW STATE, THE VOID

Three Flawed Reactions to Midlife Pressure
& The External Forces That Govern Them

THE RED PILL

Ruled by the Scoreboard

Reaction: Seeking dominance and status, letting external validation and competition decide his worth.

THE HOLLOW STATE

Ruled by the Role

Reaction: Becoming a numb performer, meeting all expectations while feeling absent and disconnected from his own life.

THE VOID

Ruled by the Critics

Reaction: Erasing himself to avoid judgment, becoming becoming invisible and agreeable to prevent any form of criticism.

Chapter 3

The Philosophy

A lighthouse stands on black rock. Waves pound from every direction. Wind howls. Night presses close. Yet the light sweeps steady circles through the dark, guiding ships that would otherwise crash. That lighthouse is the picture that captures this chapter. The Sovereign State is an inner system that keeps a man steady at the center and lets him move with power when power is needed.

Why Sovereign?

Before we go further, the word itself matters.

Sovereign means self-governing. A sovereign nation answers to no foreign power. A sovereign man answers to no external force when it comes to his internal domain. Not the scoreboard. Not the role. Not the critics. He is the rightful ruler of his own responses, his own choices, his own way of being in the world.

Sovereign in this book means self-rule over your inner state and your choices. It is personal governance, not political posture, not a quest for external dominance.

This is not arrogance. It is responsibility. A man who hands his inner kingdom to external forces is not free. He reacts. He performs. He hides. He becomes what the pressure demands instead of who he chooses to be.

The three failed paths we mapped in Chapter 2 are all surrenders of sovereignty:

The Red Pill surrenders to the scoreboard. Status rules. Competition rules. The man becomes a subject of external validation, endlessly chasing a number that someone else controls.

The Hollow State surrenders to the role. The expectation rules. The performance rules. The man becomes a subject of duty, executing tasks while his inner kingdom sits empty.

The Void surrenders entirely. Criticism rules. Judgment rules. Rather than risk ruling poorly, the man abdicates the throne altogether. Safety through absence.

The Sovereign State is the claim that you can rule yourself. Not perfectly. Not without struggle. But from a foundation that holds when external pressures surge.

That foundation is center.

The Sovereign State Defined

The Sovereign State is a way of being built on self-rule. It is an adaptable framework for middle-aged masculinity. Not a fixed picture. Not a single ideal. A method for staying the same person in many rooms while you adjust to real conditions.

At its core, the Sovereign State rests on one foundational element: center.

Center is the grounded state where self-rule becomes possible. It is body, mind, and emotion aligned. When these three line up, you can pause, feel the ground, and choose your next step without panic. You act from intention, not reaction.

Without center, sovereignty is just a word. You can claim self-rule all you want, but if your body is tense, your mind is spinning, and your emotions are flooding, you cannot govern yourself. You react. You perform. You hide. The claim becomes hollow.

From center, two capacities become available: the Eye and the Storm. These are not tools you pick up. They are what seeing and acting look like when you are grounded. A man knocked off center cannot access either one well. His sight gets cloudy. His force turns reactive. From center, both become clear.

One more thing before we go deeper. This framework is value-neutral. It does not tell you what is good. It helps you see clearly and choose deliberately. Pair it with your ethics, faith, or moral code. This framework does not replace those. It sharpens your ability to act on them.

The Behavioral Objective

Every framework needs a clear objective.

The Sovereign State is designed to help middle-aged men consistently move from external reactive to internal directed. That shift is the work.

External Reactive Mode

External reactive means your behavior, attention, and emotional state are primarily shaped by stimuli outside yourself.

The primary driver is what happens to you. Control sits outside. Other people, environments, events, and systems govern your state. Decision pattern: respond first, interpret later. Often automatic.

How it feels: swings. Irritation, urgency, validation seeking, defensiveness, spikes and drops. The attention pattern is fragmented. Pulled by notifications, people, conflict, novelty, pressure.

Listen for the phrases. You say them or think them when you are in this mode:

"I had to deal with..."

"They made me feel..."

"I couldn't focus because..."

"Once this settles down, then I can..."

The typical outcomes are energy drain, loss of strategic clarity, overcommitment, boundary erosion, and mistaking motion for progress.

External reactive has its place. True emergencies need it. Acute safety situations need it. Time-bound crisis response needs it. The problem is not the mode itself. The problem is living there by default.

Living in external reactive mode by default turns life into a reaction loop. You are governed, not governing.

Internal Directed Mode

Internal directed means your behavior, attention, and emotional state are guided by an internally chosen aim and center, regardless of external conditions.

The primary driver is what you intend. Control sits inside. Values, priorities, chosen aims. Decision pattern: orient first, then act. Response is deliberate.

How it feels: steady. Calm intensity, clarity, measured engagement. The attention pattern is sustained. Narrow when needed, broad by choice.

Listen for the phrases. You say them or think them when you are in this mode:

"Given my aim, the next move is..."

"That is noted, not decisive."

"This does not require my energy."

"I will engage here and disengage there."

The typical outcomes are energy efficiency, predictable execution, clean boundaries, compounding progress, and reduced ambiguity for others.

Internal directed is useful for leadership, long-term building, high social complexity, identity-level work, and any domain that is not an emergency. It is where you want to live most of your waking hours.

The failure mode is real. If internal directed becomes rigid or dogmatic, it can disconnect from reality. The correction is awareness, not reactivity.

The Pivot Point

The shift between these modes happens at one moment only. The pause between what happens and how you respond. That pause is where sovereignty exists.

External reactive collapses the pause. Something happens, you react. No gap. No choice. Just automatic response.

Internal directed expands the pause. Something happens, you pause, you orient to your aim, you choose, then you act. The gap creates room for governance.

Training is not about eliminating emotion or ignoring reality. It is about inserting intent before action. The pause is where you do that.

The Objective Stated

Most men shift between the two modes. Under pressure, they slide toward external reactive. In calm, they drift back toward internal directed. The shifting is constant. That is normal.

The objective of the Sovereign State is simple: reduce how often you get knocked into reactive mode and increase the time spent internally directed.

This is not a destination you reach. It is a pattern you strengthen. Over time, you spend more hours governed from inside and fewer hours governed from outside. That is the measurable change. That is the goal.

How the Three Paths Map

Now look at the three failed paths through this lens:

Red Pill is external reactive locked to status threats. The scoreboard governs. Every interaction triggers a response based on rank and dominance. The man is not choosing. He is reacting to his position in an endless competition.

Hollow State is external reactive locked to expectations. The role governs. Every task triggers automatic performance. The man is not choosing. He is reacting to what others expect of him.

Void is external reactive locked to criticism. The critics govern. Every potential judgment triggers retreat. The man is not choosing. He is reacting to avoid being seen.

Sovereign State is internal directed from center. You govern. Your aim guides your action. External events are noted, assessed, and addressed from a chosen position. You are not reacting. You are responding with intent.

Eye and Storm: The Capacities of the Centered State

Look at a satellite image of a hurricane. You see a tight circle in the middle where the sky is clear. That circle is the eye. Around it spins a massive wall of wind that tears through everything in its path. Both exist together. One does not leave the other.

This gives us the two capacities of the Sovereign State.

The Eye: Centered Seeing

The Eye is calm observation that is available to you because you are grounded. Inside that space, your breath stays slow, muscles relax, and mind sees events without distortion. From steady footing you can weigh options, note risks, and decide whether to move. Without this inner calm, choices turn sloppy and reactive.

From center, two questions become clear before every move: What is real here? What serves the aim? These questions cut through noise. They check facts against your values. They keep you from chasing image or comfort when the mission needs something else. The Eye is not passive watching. It is active judgment that prepares decisive action.

The Eye is also how you stay internal directed under pressure. Before action, it asks four questions:

First, what is my current aim?

Second, is this thing relevant to that aim?

Third, what level of engagement does it actually require?

Fourth, what happens if I do nothing for now?

If you cannot answer these questions immediately, you are likely in external reactive mode. Internal directed behavior begins when those questions precede action, not follow it. This is the practical check. Run it often.

The Storm: Centered Force

The Storm is decisive action that is available to you because you are grounded. You raise your voice to defend a colleague facing unfair blame. You make a tough financial call to protect your family. You run toward danger rather than away. The Storm uses power in service of clear intent. It comes from the core, hits the target, and then settles again.

Centered force is not wild rage. It is sized force. The volume, speed, and edge match what the moment actually needs. Too much force in a quiet moment breaks things. Too little force in a crisis wastes the opening. The Eye reads the need. The Storm delivers the dose.

Here is a guardrail worth marking. Authority is not dominance. Dominance is force for status. It seeks to win, to rank, to prove. Authority is force sized to the stakes, grounded in purpose, and clean in execution. It seeks to serve the aim, not the ego. The Storm is authority. It is decisive action that fits the moment. If you find yourself using force to prove something, you have left center.

The Relationship Between Them

Eye and Storm are not tools you pick up when needed. They are capacities that exist within the centered state. When you use the Eye, you remain centered. When you use the Storm, you remain centered. They are expressions of grounded being, not departures from it.

A man knocked off center has access to neither. His "calm" is numbness or withdrawal. His "force" is reactive control or desperate effort. Without center, he reacts instead of responds.

Problems rise when a man leans too far in one direction. If he clings only to observation, he drifts. He sees trouble coming yet hesitates. People describe him as calm but passive. At work this looks like a manager who never makes the decisive hire. At home it is a father who listens but never sets direction.

Leaning only into force flips the error. The man moves fast and loud in every situation. He turns every meeting into a clash. His family tenses at his footsteps. Constant force eats energy and trust. Over time his circle shrinks as people pull away.

The balance comes from center. Grounded seeing anchors grounded force. Grounded force protects grounded seeing.

Together they form a rhythm: observe, decide, act, reset. The Eye grants patience and clarity. The Storm provides motion and resolve. When these two capacities work in tandem, a man becomes both safe harbor and decisive actor.

The Four Principles

Think of a building. Foundation, pillars, roof. The Sovereign State rests on four pillars. Together they hold up the inner stance you need. Each pillar speaks to a habit of mind and body that shapes every choice.

Presence

Presence means you notice what is happening inside and around you without judgment. You feel the chair under you, spot tension in your shoulders, see the expression on a partner's face before words form. Presence is clear perception in real time. A man who lacks presence walks through rooms but misses signals. Misread cues turn small issues into big messes.

Intent

Intent answers "Why am I about to move?" and cuts away noise. Without clear intent, actions drift toward shallow goals like quick praise or short comfort. Intent focuses energy like a lens focuses light. It aligns choices with deeper values rather than quick emotion. When intent leads, time and talent stop leaking into tasks that do not fit your aim.

Adaptation

Life rarely sticks to the script. Markets shift, families grow, health changes. Adaptation is readiness to bend without cracking. It respects core values while adjusting tactics. Many men confuse adaptation with weakness. Oak trees that cannot flex snap in strong winds. Bamboo bends and stands back up. Adaptation means you hold your direction steady while letting form shift.

Integration

Integration pulls strength, empathy, and reason into one current. Some men pride themselves only on force. Others stay stuck in feelings. A few drift in endless analysis. Integration says each part has a seat at the table. Strength provides courage to act. Empathy reads context. Reason checks facts. When these forces align, decisions flow.

Consider how the pillars fit together. Presence spots a brewing argument before it explodes. Intent reminds you why the relationship matters. Adaptation lets you shift the conversation rather than hold a losing stance. Integration combines calm strength, patient listening, and clear logic to steer toward resolution. Missing any pillar weakens the others.

These principles form the silent architecture of the Sovereign State. Every stable action relies on them. Picture them as four corners of a square platform. Knock one corner out and the platform tilts. Keep all four corners firm and complex moves become steady.

The Triangle: Body, Mind, Emotion Aligned

The Triangle is body, mind, and emotion working as one system. When these three corners line up, that alignment is center. This is not abstract. You can feel the difference between scattered and aligned just like you can feel the difference between a wobbling wheel and a balanced one.

Think of it as governing a kingdom. You cannot govern well if you do not know what is happening inside the walls. The Triangle is your awareness of the kingdom's state. Body tells you about resources and readiness. Mind tells you about threats and priorities. Emotion tells you about stakes and values. When all three report clearly, you can rule. When any one is muted or flooding, governance fails.

Body Corner

A centered body feels stable and alive at once. Muscles ready but not clenched. Weight distributed. Attention focused. Like a sprinter in the blocks. You can feel the difference between frozen tension and ready presence. One locks the joints. The other loads the springs.

Mind Corner

A centered mind feels like one clear thought instead of ten competing voices. The aim sits plain in your head. You can name it in a short phrase. Extra thoughts still surface but they slide past instead of covering the main line. Focus feels narrow enough to act yet wide enough to adjust when new facts arrive.

Emotion Corner

Centered emotion feels settled. If anger is present, it holds shape and heat but does not spill. If concern sits in the chest, it stays clear rather than flooding the throat. The emotional field feels like water in a glass, not water on the floor. You can move the glass without wasting the content. Emotion fuels expression with honest tone rather than hijacking the moment.

When body, mind, and emotion agree, you feel a quiet click. That click is center. That is where self-rule becomes real. From center, the Eye is available. You can see clearly because nothing internal distracts. From center, the Storm is available. You can act decisively because all three corners push in the same direction.

The Triangle is the operating system for everything else. Direction without the Triangle is just a wish. Seeing without the Triangle is just guessing. Force without the Triangle is just noise. Get the Triangle aligned and everything else becomes possible.

The Triangle also guards against the three failed paths. Presence counters the Void by keeping you awake to your own life. Intent thwarts the Hollow State by tying tasks to meaning. Adaptation balances the Red Pill urge to overcontrol. Integration weaves the best parts of each path while screening out their downsides.

Purpose Over Perfection

One more foundational concept anchors the Sovereign State. Perfection is a finish line that shifts each time you draw near. Purpose is a compass that keeps pointing even when the trail twists. When you live for perfection, you overanalyze, delay, and judge every move. Purpose frees you to step, check, and adjust because the aim is direction, not flawlessness.

Purpose is made of three things. First, what you stand for: your values, the lines you will not cross, the qualities you bring to every room. Second, what you are building toward: your direction, not a fixed destination, but a trajectory. Third, who you serve beyond yourself: your contribution to family, team, or community.

Purpose also works at two levels. The long arc is your overarching direction in life. It answers: What am I here for? What does my life add up to? The present moment is what matters right here, right now, in this room. It answers: What is the aim of this conversation, this decision, this day? When the Eye asks "What serves the aim?" it is checking present-moment purpose. That present-moment purpose should align with your long arc. When they align, your small moves add up to something.

Consider work. A perfection mindset says your next project must be spotless. You spend extra hours polishing slides no one will read. Purpose asks: Will this serve the core goal? If yes, finish it and move forward. Extra polish that adds no value is weight you drop.

Think about health. A perfection lens says if you miss one workout, the whole plan is broken. So when life throws a curve you quit for days. Purpose sees the same gap and says, "Fine. Do a shorter routine now, return to schedule tomorrow." Progress continues because purpose pulls you back on course.

This shift guards against the three default traps. The Red Pill clamps down because it fears weakness. Purpose says measured progress beats harsh control. The Hollow State drifts because it sees no spark. Purpose injects meaning. The Void fades because scrutiny feels risky. Purpose offers a stable reason to act even when applause is uncertain.

Purpose over perfection is not permission to be sloppy. It is permission to be human. It lets you take the next step today with the resources you have today, knowing that the step matters more than waiting for perfect conditions that never arrive.

Closing: The Foundation Is Set

The philosophy is now in place.

Sovereign means self-governing. The Sovereign State is the claim that you can rule yourself, from a foundation that holds when external pressures surge.

The behavioral objective is clear. Move from external reactive to internal directed. Get knocked off center less often. Spend more time governed from inside.

That foundation is center: body, mind, and emotion aligned. Center is where self-rule becomes real.

From center, two capacities become available. The Eye is centered seeing. The Storm is centered force. Neither is a tool you pick up. Both are expressions of the grounded state.

Four principles hold the structure steady: presence, intent, adaptation, integration. Purpose guides the direction while perfection no longer blocks the path.

External reactive is being moved. Internal directed is choosing movement. That is the shift. That is the work.

This chapter defined what the Sovereign State is. The next chapter shows what living from center actually looks like.

Remember the lighthouse. Pressure all around. Calm center. Focused beam cutting through darkness. That is the life this framework offers. Not perfect. Not painless. But steady, purposeful, and your own.

FROM REACTION TO INTENTION: THE SOVEREIGN STATE

EXTERNAL REACTIVE MODE

INTERNAL DIRECTED MODE

Controlled by the Outside.
Your behavior, attention, and emotional state are shaped by what happens to you.

Feels Scattered & Drained.
Characterized by irritation, urgency, defensiveness, and fragmented focus.

Sounds Like: "I Had To..."
Common phrases include "They made me feel..." or "I couldn't focus because..."

THE PIVOT: HOW TO SHIFT

Master the Pause.
Sovereignty exists in the gap between an event and your response. Expand that pause to choose your action with intent.

Find Your Center.
A centered state—where Body, Mind, and Emotion are aligned—is the foundation for clear seeing and decisive action.

Guided from the Inside.
Your behavior, attention, and emotional state are guided by your chosen aim, regardless of conditions.

Feels Steady & Focused.
Characterized by calm intensity, clarity, and sustained, deliberate attention.

Sounds Like: "The Move Is..."
Common phrases include "Given my aim, the next move is..." or "This does not require my energy."

Chapter 4

The Science

A man sits in traffic after a hard day. His phone buzzes. He glances down. An email from his boss, short and sharp. By the time the light turns green, his jaw is tight, his grip on the wheel has gone white, and his shoulders have climbed toward his ears. He has not decided to be angry. He has not weighed the situation. His body made the call before his mind caught up.

This scene plays out a thousand ways. A comment from your wife lands wrong and you snap before you know why. A coworker's tone in a meeting sends heat up your neck. Your teenager rolls her eyes and something in your chest locks down. You react first. You think second. And by the time thought arrives, it is not steering. It is explaining. It is building a case for what the body already started.

Your body moves faster than your thoughts. If you want to govern yourself under pressure, you have to work with that speed, not against it. This is not philosophy. This is how the hardware works. And understanding the hardware changes what you expect from yourself when life gets loud.

The Body Gets There First

Watch what happens when threat appears. Real or imagined, the sequence is the same.

Heart rate shifts. Muscles tighten or go slack. Breathing changes. Blood moves toward the limbs or pools in the core. All of this happens in milliseconds, before conscious thought forms. The nervous system reads the environment and responds. The mind shows up later with a story to match.

This is not a flaw. It kept your ancestors alive. The ones who paused to think about the predator got eaten. The ones who moved first survived. Your nervous system carries that inheritance. It scans for threat constantly and mobilizes resources before you have a chance to weigh options.

The problem is that modern threats rarely need a physical response. A tense email is not a predator. A hard conversation with your wife is not a fight for survival. But the nervous system does not know the difference. It reads tone, posture, facial expression, and context. It mobilizes anyway. Heart rate climbs. Muscles brace. Vision narrows. The body prepares for battle while you sit in a chair or stand in your kitchen.

Here is what this means. If the body is signaling danger, the mind will believe it. It will find reasons to justify the alarm. Anxiety builds a case for worry. Anger builds a case for offense. Withdrawal builds a case for retreat. The man thinks the problem is the situation. Often the problem is the state he was in when he met it.

You have felt this. You walked into a conversation already activated from something else. The conversation went badly. Later you realized the other person did not do anything unusual.

You were already primed. The fuse was already laid. They just lit it.

This is why you cannot think your way into calm once the system has already fired. By the time you form the argument, physiology has locked in. You are trying to steer a car that already left the road.

The Loop That Runs You

Psychology used to treat the mind as the driver and the body as the passenger. Think different thoughts. Feel different feelings. The body will follow. This works, but only within a certain range. If your nervous system is already in full alarm, no amount of positive self-talk will settle it.

Somatic psychology reversed the direction. It treats the body as the faster, more reliable lever. Change your breathing. Shift your posture. Release the tension in your jaw. The nervous system reads those signals and adjusts. Thoughts and emotions follow.

The truth is that neither direction rules in all cases. They form a loop.

A thought can start a physical cascade. You read bad news about your industry. Your stomach drops. Your chest tightens. Your shoulders creep up. The body responds to what the mind perceived.

A physical state can shape what you think and feel. You sit hunched at a desk for hours. Energy drains. Mood sours. Thoughts turn negative without any new information arriving. The mind is explaining what the body is already doing.

You have lived in this loop without naming it. The days when your body felt heavy and your thoughts followed it down. The moments when a worry took root and your chest tightened for hours. The times you felt fine until you noticed your shoulders were at your ears, and then suddenly you did not feel fine at all.

The loop runs whether you watch it or not. Watching it changes what becomes possible.

Three Gears

Your autonomic nervous system runs in different modes. Think of them as gears. Each gear feels different in the body and produces different behavior.

In the calm gear, your heart beats steadily. Breath runs slow and low in the belly. Muscles carry only the tension the moment actually requires. The prefrontal cortex, the planning and decision-making part of the brain, is fully online. You can weigh options. You can delay reactions. You can see the larger picture.

This is where choice lives. This is where self-rule becomes possible.

In the threat gear, the body mobilizes for action. Heart rate spikes. Breathing moves up into the chest and quickens. Blood flows to the limbs. The brain shifts toward speed and away from nuance. Fine motor control drops. Complex thinking narrows. This gear is useful when you need to run or fight. It is not useful when you need to have a hard conversation with your wife or make a careful decision about your career.

In the shutdown gear, the system goes flat. Energy drains. Motivation disappears. The body is trying to minimize damage by disengaging. This gear looks like depression or numbness. The man is still present, but barely. He has left the field to protect himself from further loss.

You know these gears. You have lived in each one.

You know what threat gear feels like. The meeting that left you buzzing for hours. The argument that kept your chest tight through dinner. The news that sent your heart racing and kept it there long after the information was old.

You know what shutdown gear feels like. The Sunday afternoon when you could not make yourself do anything. The stretch of weeks when nothing seemed to matter. The flatness that arrived after a loss and stayed longer than it should have.

You know what calm gear feels like too, even if you spend less time there than you would like. The morning when everything felt manageable. The conversation that flowed without effort. The decision that came clearly because nothing inside was fighting it.

Most men move through these gears all day without noticing. Coffee pushes toward activation. Arguments push toward threat. Defeat or boredom push toward shutdown. The gears shift on their own while the man thinks he is making choices.

Here is a scene. A father comes home after a hard day. His body is still running in threat gear from a tense meeting. His teenager asks for money. The father snaps. The reaction is too big for the moment. Later he wonders why he lost his temper over nothing. The answer is that his nervous system was already primed. The kid just lit a fuse that was already laid.

You have been that father. Maybe not with a teenager. But you have snapped at someone who did not deserve it because your body was already running hot from something else. You have shut down on someone who needed you because your system was already in conservation mode. The gear you were in shaped what happened next.

What You Stopped Noticing

There is a technical word for the ability to sense internal body signals. Psychologists call it interoception. It means noticing tension, warmth, pressure, heartbeat, or breath without outside prompts.

Most men have let this capacity atrophy.

There was a time when you knew what you felt in your body. As a child, you knew when you were hungry, tired, scared, or excited. The signals were clear. You responded to them.

Then life trained you to override the signals. Push through the fatigue. Ignore the tension. Keep going when your body said stop. The signals did not disappear. You just stopped listening. After enough years of not listening, the signals got quieter. Or you got deaf to them.

Now you blow up at your wife and wonder why. You drag through a weekend and call it exhaustion. You make a bad decision and only later realize you were not thinking clearly because your body was in threat mode the whole time. You live at the mercy of forces you never see coming because you stopped reading the dashboard.

Think of a car with no gauges. No speedometer. No fuel indicator. No temperature warning. You drive until something breaks. Then you react. Most men live this way internally. They have no read on their own state until it is already too late to adjust.

The good news is that this capacity is not gone. It is dormant. Men who start paying attention find that the signals come back. The connection rebuilds. The dashboard lights up again.

This matters because early signals give you room. You feel the first flutter of anger before it becomes a blast. You notice the tightening in your chest before it becomes a full shutdown. Early signals mean early choice. Late signals mean cleanup.

What This Means for Sovereignty

Philosophy alone does not change reactions. You can believe in self-rule and still lose your temper in traffic. You can want to govern yourself and still shut down when your wife raises her voice. The gap between intention and action is not a character flaw. It is a nervous system problem.

This is why the Sovereign State framework treats the body as infrastructure, not afterthought.

Sovereignty is the philosophical claim. Self-rule. The authority to govern your own responses, choices, and way of being. But a claim without capacity is just a wish.

The capacity comes from working with the body. When you can shift your nervous system from threat gear into calm gear, the prefrontal cortex comes back online. You can think. You can choose. You can act with intention instead of reacting from momentum.

This is not about becoming emotionless. It is about having range. The ability to feel anger without being hijacked by it. The ability to face threat without collapsing or exploding. The ability to stay present in hard moments instead of checking out.

The nervous system is not fixed. The gears become easier to notice. The capacity to shift them grows with attention. A man who works with his physiology instead of against it builds a different kind of stability over time.

Purpose matters here too. Regulation without direction is just self-soothing. You can calm down and still drift. You can settle your nervous system and still have no idea what you are building. The framework links regulation to purpose so that the calm gear serves movement, not just comfort.

Adaptability is the proof that the system works. When you can enter different rooms, face different pressures, absorb different setbacks, and still keep moving, something has changed. The capacity to stay grounded travels with you because it lives in the body, not in the circumstances.

The Hardware and the Choice

Three things matter here.

First, your body reacts faster than your thoughts. This is not a problem to fix. It is a fact to work with. The man who expects willpower to override physiology will keep losing. The man who learns to work with the body has a different experience.

Second, the gears are not fixed. You are not stuck in threat mode or shutdown mode. The nervous system responds to input. Attention changes what is possible. Men who could not sit still at forty find a different capacity at fifty because they started paying attention to what their body was doing.

Third, regulation without aim is incomplete. The goal is not to feel calm. The goal is to govern yourself while moving toward something that matters. The science provides the mechanism. The philosophy provides the direction. Both matter.

When you understand how the hardware works, you stop blaming yourself for reactions that happened before thought could intervene. You stop expecting willpower to win every fight. You start working with the system instead of against it.

You also start to recognize what was happening in all those moments that confused you. The snap that came from nowhere. The shutdown that lasted too long. The decision that made no sense in hindsight. The hardware was doing what hardware does. Now you know.

The next chapter shows what this looks like when it comes together. The grounded state where self-rule becomes real. The capacities that flow from it. The science you just learned explains why it works. What follows is what it feels like when it does.

THE LOOP THAT RUNS YOU

1. THE TRIGGER

A "Threat" Appears

Your nervous system reads modern stressors (a sharp email, a coworker's tone) as a physical threat.

2. THE PHYSICAL RESPONSE

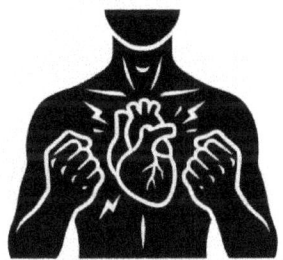

Your Body Reacts First

In milliseconds, before conscious thought, your heart rate shifts, muscles tighten, and breath changes.

4. THE LOOP LOCKS IN

The Feeling Becomes The "Truth"

The story amplifies the physical stress, making it harder to think clearly or choose your response.

3. THE MENTAL JUSTIFICATION

Your Mind Explains It

Your brain creates a story to justify the body's alarm, building a case for anger, anxiety, or retreat.

Chapter 5

The Center

There have been moments when everything lined up. A hard conversation that stayed calm. A decision that came clear without the usual spin. A stretch of hours when presence was full and action was fitted to what the moment actually needed. Body steady. Mind quiet. Emotion present but not flooding.

These moments were not planned. They happened. And when they passed, something was different. The usual noise had gone quiet. Reactions that normally fired on their own did not fire. There was space to see, space to choose, space to act from somewhere solid.

That state has a name. It is center.

What Center Is

Center is the aligned state of body, mind, and emotion that lets a man choose instead of react. It is not a mood. It is not a feeling. It is a condition of the system.

When the body is settled, the mind is clear, and emotion is fitted to the moment, something clicks into place. The usual static drops away. What is real becomes visible. What serves the aim becomes obvious. Action becomes possible without the drag of internal conflict.

This is not mystical. It is mechanical. The nervous system has a state where threat signals quiet and the thinking brain comes online. Breath slows. Muscles release their grip. The field of vision widens. Options appear that were invisible a moment before.

Center is that state, recognized and named.

What Center Feels Like

In the body, center feels like weight that has found its proper place. Feet solid on the floor. Shoulders down and back, not braced but not collapsed. Jaw unclenched. Breath low in the belly, not high in the chest. There is readiness without tension. The body is available for action but not activated for threat.

The opposite is familiar. Shoulders at the ears. Jaw tight. Breath shallow. Weight forward, as if already leaning into the next fight. Or weight collapsed, as if the fight is already lost. Center is neither of these. It is the body at rest and ready at the same time.

In the mind, center feels like one clear signal instead of competing noise. The aim is visible. Thoughts arise but they do not pile up. There is focus without strain. Attention can be placed and held without constant effort.

The opposite is also familiar. Spinning on a problem without resolution. Jumping from thought to thought without landing. Trying to focus while something underneath keeps pulling away. Center is none of these. It is the mind with room to see.

In emotion, center feels like contact without flooding. Feeling is present but it does not run the show. Anger can be there without explosion. Concern can be there without paralysis. Joy can be there without manic scatter. The emotion fits the situation. It fuels action instead of hijacking it.

The opposite is well known. Reaction that overshoots the trigger. Numbness that blocks access to any feeling at all. Mood that shifts with every input. Center is none of these. It is emotion in range, available for use.

When all three align, the click is unmistakable. This is the territory from which governance becomes possible.

The Hub

Think of center as the hub of a wheel.

The spokes are roles. Worker. Partner. Parent. Friend. Leader. Follower. Each spoke connects to the outer rim where life happens. But all the spokes meet at the hub. If the hub is solid, the wheel can take impact and keep rolling. If the hub is weak, the spokes wobble and the whole thing shakes apart.

A life built on the spokes alone is fragile. Identity tied to the job collapses when the job changes. Identity tied to the relationship fractures when the relationship strains. Identity tied to performance crumbles when performance slips.

Center is identity that lives in the hub. The spokes can change. Roles can shift. Seasons can turn. The hub holds because it does not depend on any single spoke. A man can lose a title, end a chapter, watch a role fade, and still know who he is. The wheel keeps turning because the center holds.

This is not theory. It is felt. The difference between reacting from a role and responding from center is obvious in the moment. One feels precarious. The other feels solid. One requires the external situation to hold steady. The other holds steady regardless.

What Pulls You Out

Center is not a permanent state. It is a home base. Life pulls away from it constantly.

External pressure knocks men off center every day. A deadline tightens. A conflict escalates. An expectation lands that cannot be met. The body activates. The mind speeds up. Emotion floods or flattens. Center disappears without a conscious departure.

Old patterns have their own gravity. Reactions learned decades ago still fire on cue. A tone of voice triggers defensiveness. A certain look triggers withdrawal. A type of situation triggers the same failed response, again. These patterns pull away from center before awareness even registers what happened.

Fatigue degrades the system. Sleep debt, chronic stress, physical depletion. The resources required to hold center run low. What was easy becomes difficult. What was difficult becomes impossible. The drift happens slowly, then all at once.

Emotional residue accumulates. The conversation that was never finished. The loss that was never processed. The anger that was never addressed. These sit in the system and tilt it. Center becomes harder to find because something is always pulling from underneath.

None of this is failure. It is the terrain. The question is not whether drift happens. It is whether return is possible.

The Levers Already in Use

Return is not foreign. It has happened before.

The body has levers that shift state. They have been used without being named.

Breath is the most direct. A long exhale before a hard conversation. A sigh when tension finally breaks. The moment of noticing the breath was held, and letting it go. Each time, something shifted. The exhale told the nervous system the emergency was over. The system believed it.

Posture sends its own signals. Straightening up when strength was needed. Squaring the shoulders before confrontation. Standing taller when feeling small. The body knew that position changes state. It also knew the reverse. Hours of hunching made the mood drop. Curling inward deepened defeat. The body reads itself and adjusts accordingly.

Tension release clears what has accumulated. Shaking out the hands after something intense. Rolling the neck. Stretching when wound too tight. The body stores what is not discharged. Release lets it go. A clenched jaw softens. Tight fists open. Raised shoulders drop. Each release sends the signal: stand down.

Grounding pulls attention into the present through sensation. Feet on the floor when the mind was racing. Weight in the chair when everything felt unsteady. Temperature, texture, sound. These anchored awareness in the only moment that can actually be governed.

None of this was learned from a manual. The body discovered what worked when it needed to work. The levers are already known. They simply have not been named.

The Pause and the Questions

Between stimulus and response, there is sometimes a gap.

A beat before replying to the message that triggered anger. A breath between provocation and reaction. The almost-said thing that stayed unsaid. In that gap, something happened. Options appeared that would not have been visible if reaction had been immediate.

The gap has appeared before. Not through technique. Through some instinct that knew immediate reaction would make things worse.

When the pause is missing, reaction completes before choice is recognized. Words leave the mouth too fast. The email sends before better judgment arrives. Afterward, the question: why was stopping impossible? The answer: there was no space. Stimulus arrived and pattern fired.

When the pause is present, the moment stretches. The pull toward reaction is felt but not followed. What is happening becomes visible. What to do becomes a question. Choice belongs to the person, not the pattern.

In that pause, two questions cut through the noise.

What is real here? This question has been asked mid-conflict. An attempt to see whether the reaction matched what was actually happening. Sometimes the answer was humbling: the activation was larger than the situation warranted. An old wound was doing the reacting. Sometimes the answer confirmed the read: the situation was genuinely difficult. Either way, asking the question was governance. Checking the territory before acting.

What serves my aim? This question has also surfaced. What do I actually want here? What response would serve? What would I choose if the pattern was not pulling? The difference between reacting from pattern and choosing from purpose is felt. One is automatic. The other is deliberate.

The pause and the questions have appeared before. They can be found again.

The Return

Drift happens. So does return.

Drift has a feel. The day accumulates small tensions. By evening, steady is a memory and the departure point is unclear. Or something knocks sideways. A comment. A disappointment. A memory surfacing without warning. Suddenly reactive, with no clear sense of how long the absence has lasted.

Return has its own feel. The moment of noticing activation. Recognition that the pattern is running. This noticing is itself the first shift. In the pattern, then seeing the pattern. Something opens.

Return happens through the body. A breath, and the exhale settles something. Shoulders drop, and the system recalibrates. Feet on the floor, and arrival in the present. The body leads. The mind follows.

Return happens through the questions. Asking what is real and seeing the reaction was oversized. Asking what serves and seeing the pattern was serving nothing. The seeing leads. The shift follows.

Return happens fast or slow. Sometimes it takes hours to notice the drift. Sometimes it takes one breath to come back. The pathway strengthens with use. What once required effort becomes available with less.

Every return is practice. The capacity to come back is built by coming back.

What Changes When It Is Named

The levers have been used. The pause has appeared. The questions have been asked. The return has happened.

What changes when these are named is that they can be found on purpose.

The breath that calmed by accident becomes available by choice. Activation rises and what to do is known. Not because a technique was installed. Because what has worked is recognized and can be reached for deliberately.

The pause that appeared sometimes becomes available more often. The pull toward reaction is felt, and the knowledge that a gap is possible is present. It has been created before. It can be created again.

The questions that surfaced occasionally become available regularly. Reaction is felt and what to ask is known. What is real. What serves. The questions cut through noise because they have been asked before and their effect is understood.

The return that happened slowly becomes available quickly. Signs of drift are recognized earlier. The catch happens sooner. The way back is familiar. What took hours takes minutes. What took minutes takes breaths.

This is not transformation. It is recognition. What has already been done is being named, and the skill is learning to do it when it counts.

What Governance Makes Possible

A man with access to center lives differently than a man without it.

Situations that once caused collapse now get handled. Not because the situations changed. Because the man meeting them changed. He has ground to stand on. He can take the hit without losing his position.

Reactions that once ran on automatic now have a checkpoint. The pattern still arises. It does not complete without review. There is a moment to see it, evaluate it, and decide whether to let it run.

Relationships that once depended on ideal conditions now survive real ones. Conflict does not destroy the connection. Disappointment does not end the conversation. There is enough stability to absorb impact and keep going.

The gap between intention and action shrinks. What a man means to do and what he actually does move closer together. Fewer apologies are needed because fewer mistakes are made. Not perfection. Just a higher percentage of moments governed instead of reacted through.

This is not visible to the outside world. No scoreboard tracks it. But it is felt. In how the days land. In how the difficult moments resolve. In how much of life is actually lived from choice rather than pattern.

Capacity grows with use. The practice never ends because life keeps delivering material. But the return gets faster. The access gets more reliable. The percentage of governed moments increases.

The starting point was before any of this was named. Something already knew how to find center. Now it has words.

Visit Appendix B for centering practices.

The next chapter shows how purpose keeps movement going when conditions are imperfect and the path forward is unclear.

GOVERN YOURSELF

YOU ARE GOVERNED BY CONDITIONING

Your automatic reactions were trained into you by past experiences; they are not conscious choices.

SELF-GOVERNANCE IS CHOOSING YOUR RESPONSE

The goal is to build the capacity to choose how you respond, rather than letting your conditioning choose for you.

TRAIN THE PAUSE

Practice creating a gap between a trigger and your reaction to see clearly and make a deliberate choice.

IT'S NOT ABOUT PERFECTION

When you lose control, the real practice is to notice, return to center, and reclaim your governance.

Chapter 6

The Purpose

You now have center. You have the capacity to govern yourself. You can settle your body, create the pause, ask the questions, and return when you drift.

But capacity without direction is just calm drifting. A ship with a working engine and no destination still goes nowhere that matters.

This chapter is about direction. What you are governing yourself toward. What gives your self-governance shape and aim.

The answer is purpose. And the enemy of purpose is not laziness or weakness. It is perfectionism. Perfectionism masquerades as high standards. It feels like motivation. But it is actually a surrender of governance. When you chase perfection, you hand control to external standards, to fear of judgment, to what others might think. You become governed by an ideal that exists outside you rather than a direction that lives inside you.

Purpose over perfection is the choice to be internally directed rather than externally evaluated. It is choosing your aim over their scoreboard.

Why Perfection Freezes You

Perfectionism wears the mask of excellence. It tells you that you are just trying to do things right. That your standards are high because you care. That hesitation is really just careful preparation.

But look at what perfectionism actually produces. Paralysis. Delay. Half-started projects abandoned when they could not meet the ideal. Conversations avoided because you could not find the perfect words. Decisions postponed until conditions were just right. Conditions that never arrived.

Perfectionism is not about quality. It is about fear. Fear of being judged. Fear of falling short. Fear of exposure. The perfect ideal becomes a wall you hide behind. As long as you are still preparing, still refining, still waiting for the right moment, you cannot be criticized for the attempt. You cannot fail at what you never fully tried.

This is external reactive behavior dressed in respectable clothing. You are not pursuing excellence. You are managing your fear of judgment. The external world and its potential criticism is governing your choices. Your movement is controlled by what others might think, not by what you are trying to build.

A man governed by perfectionism is not free. He is trapped by standards he did not choose, evaluated by judges he cannot see, frozen by verdicts that have not been delivered and may never be.

Purpose cuts through this. Purpose says: here is the direction. Move toward it. Imperfectly. Repeatedly. Now.

Purpose as Compass

Purpose is not a destination. It is a direction.

Think of a compass in fog. You cannot see where you are going. The path is unclear. Conditions keep shifting. But the compass points north. It does not tell you exactly where to step. It tells you which way to face. You adjust your steps to the terrain, but you keep moving in the direction the compass shows.

Purpose works the same way. It does not give you a detailed map of your life. It does not tell you exactly what to do in every situation. It gives you orientation. When you are unsure, you check the compass. When conditions change, you check the compass. When you have drifted, you check the compass. The direction holds even when the path shifts.

Purpose operates on two time horizons.

Long purpose is your due north. It is what you stand for. What you are building over years and decades. Who you serve beyond yourself. This is the deep orientation that shapes your life as a whole. It might be: building a family that knows how to love well. Creating work that solves real problems. Leaving your corner of the world better than you found it. Becoming the kind of man your younger self needed to meet.

Long purpose does not change often. It is the foundation. When you make major life decisions, this is what you check against.

Immediate purpose is what this moment requires. What is your aim in this conversation? In this meeting? In this day? What does this situation need from the man you are choosing to be?

Immediate purpose changes constantly. The aim in a conflict with your wife is different from the aim in a negotiation at work. The aim when your child is struggling is different from the aim when your team needs direction. Immediate purpose is responsive. It adapts to the room.

When the two align, your small moves add up to something. Your daily choices accumulate in the direction of your long arc. This is how a life gets built. Not through one dramatic decision, but through thousands of small moves that share a direction.

When you ask "what serves my aim?" you are checking immediate purpose. But that immediate purpose should connect to your long purpose. The question keeps you internal directed. Your aim governs your response, not the stimulus.

Purpose Prevents Drift

Without clear purpose, every stimulus looks urgent. Every demand seems to require response. Every criticism lands with full weight. You bounce from one external pressure to another, reacting to whatever is loudest.

This is external reactive living. The environment governs the man. He is moved rather than moving.

Purpose acts as a filter. When you know your aim, you can sort incoming stimuli. Is this relevant to my purpose? Does this require engagement, or is it noise? Does this need action now, or can it wait? What happens if I do nothing?

Without the filter, everything gets through. With the filter, you can focus. You can give your energy to what matters and decline to spend it on what does not. This is not coldness or detachment. It is governance. You are choosing where your attention goes rather than having it pulled by whatever shows up.

Four questions test whether you are internally directed or externally reactive in any moment:

What is my current aim?

Is this stimulus relevant to that aim?

What level of engagement does it actually require?

What happens if I do nothing for now?

If you cannot answer these questions quickly, you are likely in external reactive mode. The stimulus has taken over. You are responding to pressure rather than moving from purpose.

The Trigger Audit

When you feel a pull to react, slow down. Run an audit.

Something happened. You got triggered. You are about to do something. Before you do it, ask: Where did this come from? Is this response arising from purpose, or from an old script? From clear thinking, or from fear? From what the situation requires, or from habit?

Does this response serve my purpose?

If yes, proceed. If no, ask: what would serve?

This audit takes seconds once you have practiced it. It is not endless deliberation. It is a quick check before action. Am I about to move from purpose, or react from pattern?

The audit applies to negative triggers and positive triggers equally. Anger and fear can pull you off center. So can praise, attraction, and status wins. When someone flatters you, when a victory lands, when external validation arrives, run the same audit. Does your next move serve purpose, or does it serve the feeling? Chasing the high of validation is just as reactive as fleeing the pain of criticism. Both hand governance to external forces.

Visit Appendix D for a Trigger Audit

Adaptive Strength

Purpose does not mean rigidity. The compass points north, but you still navigate around obstacles.

A tree that cannot bend breaks in the wind. A tree that bends too easily offers no shelter. The strong tree has deep roots and flexible branches. It holds its ground and adapts to conditions.

Your values are the roots. They do not move. What you stand for, what you will not compromise, what defines the man you are. These are fixed.

Your tactics are the branches. They move constantly. How you pursue your purpose in this situation, with these people, under these conditions. The approach adapts even when the aim stays constant.

Rigidity confuses values with tactics. It insists on doing things one way because that way worked before. When conditions change, rigidity breaks.

Adaptive strength knows the difference. It holds values firmly and holds tactics loosely. It asks: what does my purpose require in this specific situation? The answer today might differ from the answer yesterday. That is not weakness. That is responsiveness.

Imperfection as Data

You will miss the mark. You will act in ways that do not serve your purpose. You will react when you meant to respond. You will make choices you later see as wrong.

This is not defect. It is data.

A carpenter who hits a nail crooked does not conclude that he is incapable of carpentry. He looks at what happened. He adjusts his next swing. The bent nail is information about his technique, not a verdict on his worth.

Treat your imperfections the same way. When you drift from purpose, when you fail to live by your values, when the gap between who you want to be and how you acted becomes visible, do not collapse into shame. Shame does not improve the next swing. It just makes you avoid the hammer.

Instead, examine. What happened? What pulled you off? What pattern fired? What can you do differently next time? Record it in the logbook. Adjust. Move forward.

Repair matters more than perfection. When you harm someone, you repair. When you fail yourself, you repair. The repair is the practice. It is not evidence of failure. It is evidence of commitment. You are still in the work.

Social Gravity

Purpose has social gravity. It draws people in.

A man who knows his direction creates stability for others. His team knows what they are working toward. His family knows what he stands for. People can orient around him because he is oriented himself.

This does not mean he controls others or imposes his purpose on them. It means his clarity creates a kind of anchor. When things get chaotic, people look for something steady. A man with clear purpose offers that steadiness.

Purpose also lowers tension in groups. When everyone knows the aim, disagreements become tactical rather than existential. You are not fighting about who is right. You are figuring out how to move toward the shared direction. The purpose provides the frame that contains the conflict.

Consistency of why allows flexibility of how. When your team trusts your purpose, they give you room to adapt your methods. When your family knows what you stand for, they can tolerate changes in approach. The deep consistency frees you to be responsive on the surface.

Drift Markers

You will drift from purpose. The question is how quickly you notice.

Learn your markers. Each of the three paths has characteristic drift signs.

Red Pill drift shows as body tension that outpaces reality. You are activated, ready to fight, scanning for threats. But the actual situation does not warrant combat. Your system is responding to an imagined challenge to status, not a real one. This is external reactive to perceived threat.

Hollow State drift shows as a mind filled with shiny extras. You start chasing side projects, new ideas, distractions. You are busy but not moving toward your purpose. The activity is a way of avoiding the real work, which has become heavy or unclear. This is external reactive to expectation, performing motion without meaning.

Void drift shows as emotional flatline. You stop caring. The purpose that once moved you now seems distant or pointless. You are withdrawing, making yourself smaller, reducing your exposure. This is external reactive to the possibility of criticism. Better to aim at nothing than to aim and miss.

Watch for language shifts. When "move" becomes "should," you have drifted. "Move" is internal directed. "Should" is external reactive. When silent math starts running in the background, calculating reputation, managing perception, weighing how things look, you have drifted. Reputation math is governance by external judgment.

Catch the drift early. The sooner you notice, the easier the return.

The Scene

Your wife makes a comment about how much you have been working lately. Her tone has an edge. Something about it lands hard.

The old pattern wants to fire. Defend yourself. Explain why the work is necessary. Counter with something about her own schedule. Or absorb it silently, withdraw, let resentment build.

Both responses are external reactive. The first is governed by threat to status. The second is governed by fear of conflict. Neither serves purpose.

You catch the drift. Your shoulders have climbed. Your jaw is tight. You are about to react.

You breathe. You settle. You ask: what is my aim here? Connection. Understanding. Partnership. Not being right. Not defending your honor. Connection.

You ask: what is real here? Her tone landed hard. But what is she actually saying? What is underneath the edge? She might be lonely. She might be worried about you. She might be carrying something that has nothing to do with your work hours.

You ask: what serves my aim? Curiosity, not defense. A question, not an argument.

You respond: "That landed hard. What are you actually trying to say?"

The conversation shifts. She was not attacking. She was reaching, awkwardly. Now you are talking instead of defending. Connection becomes possible.

No damage done. No repair needed. The pattern was interrupted before it could run. Internal directed held.

Purpose and the Triangle

Purpose lives in all three corners of the Triangle.

Body supports purpose through energy and capacity. A depleted body cannot pursue much of anything. Physical stability gives you the resources to move toward your aim.

Mind supports purpose through clarity and planning. You need to see the path, break it into steps, navigate obstacles. Mental clarity keeps you oriented.

Emotion supports purpose through meaning and fuel. Purpose without feeling is dry and fragile. The emotional connection to your aim is what makes it worth pursuing. It is what gets you up when you fall.

When all three corners align around purpose, you have coherence. Body, mind, and emotion pointing the same direction. This is what integrated movement feels like. Not three parts in conflict, but one system moving as a whole.

When the corners conflict, purpose fragments. Your body is exhausted but your mind is pushing harder. Your emotions are checked out but you keep going through the motions. These misalignments are signals. They tell you that something in the Triangle needs attention before you can move well.

The Direction

Purpose is not a luxury. It is what makes self-governance meaningful.

Without purpose, you have capacity with no direction. You can govern yourself, but toward what? The vacuum fills with whatever external pressure is loudest.

With purpose, your governance has shape. Your choices accumulate. Your small moves build. You are not just managing yourself. You are building something.

Perfection is the enemy because it hands evaluation to external judges. Purpose is the answer because it returns governance to you. You set the aim. You move toward it. You adjust when you drift. You continue.

The compass does not care about the fog. It points north regardless. Your purpose works the same way. Conditions shift. The path is unclear. The direction holds.

The next chapter shows how to adapt when circumstances change without losing your center or your aim.

PURPOSE OVER PERFECTION

PERFECTION IS A TRAP

It masquerades as high standards but is actually fear of judgment that freezes you in place.

PURPOSE IS YOUR COMPASS

It doesn't provide a detailed map, but a constant direction to orient yourself, especially in uncertainty.

PURPOSE IS A FILTER

It helps you distinguish between what truly matters and what is merely noise, preventing a reactive life.

TREAT IMPERFECTION AS DATA

A misstep isn't a verdict on your worth; it's information you can use to adjust and improve your next attempt.

Chapter 7

The Adaptability

A ship with a fixed rudder cannot navigate. It can only go where the wind pushes it. When conditions change, it has no response. It is at the mercy of forces outside itself.

A ship with no rudder at all is worse. It spins with every wave. It has no direction at all. Movement without orientation.

The sovereign man is neither. He has a rudder. He uses it. He adjusts to conditions while maintaining his heading. The wind shifts. The current pulls. He responds. But he responds in service of his direction, not in surrender to the forces around him.

This is adaptability. Not rigidity that breaks. Not compliance that drifts. The capacity to move with conditions while staying governed from the inside.

Adaptability Defined

Adaptability is not compromise. Compromise means giving up part of what you want. Adaptability means finding a different way to get there.

Adaptability is not surrender. Surrender means the external forces won. Adaptability means you are still in command, choosing your response based on what the situation actually requires.

Adaptability is not becoming external reactive to fit the room. That is a different thing entirely. When you reshape yourself to match expectations, when you abandon your aim to avoid friction, when you let the environment dictate who you are, you have not adapted. You have capitulated. The room is governing you.

True adaptability is staying internal directed while adjusting your tactics to match real conditions. Your aim holds. Your method shifts. The difference matters.

A man who insists on one approach regardless of circumstances is not strong. He is brittle. He mistakes stubbornness for principle. When the situation changes, he either breaks or becomes irrelevant.

A man who changes his aim whenever he meets resistance is not flexible. He is lost. He mistakes compliance for adaptation. He ends up wherever the pressure pushes him, with no direction of his own.

The sovereign man holds his aim and adjusts his approach. He reads the room. He assesses conditions. He chooses the method that serves his purpose in this specific context. Tomorrow the method might change. The purpose remains.

Adapting Without Losing Center

Center makes adaptability possible.

Without center, change feels threatening. Every shift in conditions triggers a defensive response. You grip tighter on your current approach because letting go feels like losing control. Or you collapse entirely, abandoning your position because holding it has become too costly. Neither is adaptation. Both are reactions.

From center, you can hold steady and move at the same time. You have the stability to observe changing conditions without being destabilized by them. You can ask: what does this situation actually require? What approach would serve my purpose here? You can consider options because you are not in survival mode.

This is the paradox. Steadiness enables change. The more grounded you are, the more freely you can move. The less you grip your current position, the more options you have.

Think of a martial artist. His center of gravity is low and stable. From that stability, he can move in any direction. He can respond to whatever his opponent does. His rootedness is what makes his mobility possible. If he were off balance, he would have to fight just to stay standing. From balance, he can fight to win.

Your center works the same way. When you are grounded, change is a choice. When you are ungrounded, change is a threat. Adaptability requires the foundation that center provides.

Adaptability Across the Triangle

Adaptability shows up in all three corners of the Triangle. Each corner has its own form of flexibility.

Physical adaptability is the body's capacity to adjust. Energy management across different demands. Pacing yourself for a long day versus sprinting for a deadline. Adjusting your physical presence to match the room. Standing tall in one context, sitting back in another. Reading what the situation needs from your body and providing it.

Physical adaptability also means knowing your limits and working with them. The body you have today may not be the body you had ten years ago. Adaptation means adjusting your expectations and methods to match your actual capacity, not the capacity you wish you had.

Mental adaptability is the mind's capacity to shift frames. Seeing a problem from multiple angles. Updating your understanding when new information arrives. Letting go of a plan that is not working and generating a new one. Holding your conclusions loosely enough that reality can correct them.

Mental adaptability is not weakness of conviction. It is strength of thinking. A mind that cannot change is not disciplined. It is stuck. The sovereign man can hold a position firmly and release it cleanly when the evidence demands it.

Emotional adaptability is the capacity to feel what the situation calls for without being hijacked. Bringing warmth to a conversation that needs connection. Bringing seriousness to a moment that requires gravity. Allowing yourself to feel grief when loss arrives, then returning to function when function is required.

Emotional adaptability is not suppression. Suppression locks emotions in place. Adaptability lets them move. You feel what arises. You let it inform you. And then you choose how to respond based on what serves your purpose, not just what the emotion is pushing for.

The three corners support each other. Physical groundedness makes mental clarity possible. Mental clarity helps you understand your emotions. Emotional awareness tells you what matters in the situation. When all three are adapting together, you move as a whole person. When one corner is stuck, the others compensate, but at a cost.

When to Adapt, When to Hold

Not everything should bend. The question is always: what stays fixed and what can move?

Purpose is the test. Does this adaptation serve your aim, or abandon it? If changing your approach moves you toward your purpose, adapt. If the change means giving up on your purpose to avoid discomfort, hold. The purpose is the compass. Check it before you shift.

Values are the lines. Some things are not negotiable. What you stand for, what you will not do, what defines the man you are. These are the boundaries of adaptation. You can change methods endlessly. You cannot change values without becoming someone else. Know where your lines are. When adaptation would cross a line, hold.

Capacity is the guard. Adaptation requires resources. Energy, attention, emotional bandwidth. If you are depleted, your capacity to adapt wisely is compromised. Sometimes holding your current position is the right move simply because you do not have the reserves to navigate a change well. Protect your capacity. It is what makes future adaptation possible.

Relationships are the check. Adaptation affects other people. When you change your approach, others have to adjust too. If your adaptations are constant and unpredictable, people cannot trust you. They do not know which version of you they are getting. Check your adaptations against your relationships. Are you being responsive, or are you being chaotic?

Signals You Are Off Course

Adaptation can slide into reaction without you noticing. The shift is subtle. You think you are being flexible, but you have actually become unmoored.

Learn the warning signs.

Body signals. Tension that does not match the situation. Fatigue that comes from constant shapeshifting. The feeling of performing rather than being. When your body is working hard to maintain an adaptation, something is off. True adaptation feels more easeful than that.

Mind signals. Confusion about what you actually think. Difficulty remembering what you decided and why. A sense of being scattered, with too many approaches running at once. When your mind cannot track your own positions, you have likely drifted from adaptation into reactivity.

Emotion signals. Resentment that builds quietly. The feeling of abandoning yourself. Anger at others for expectations you chose to meet. When adaptation leaves an emotional residue of self-betrayal, you have crossed a line somewhere.

Language signals. When you cannot explain why you shifted, you probably reacted rather than adapted. When you become defensive about a change, you are likely protecting a choice you are not sure about. When you find yourself justifying rather than explaining, something has slipped.

Relationship signals. When others seem confused by your inconsistency. When trust erodes because people do not know what to expect. When you get feedback that you are hard to read, that people do not know where you stand. These signals suggest your adaptation has become unreliability.

External reactive warning signs. Four specific patterns indicate you have slipped from adapting to reacting:

You changed your aim, not just your method. True adaptation keeps the destination and changes the route. If you find that your purpose itself has shifted to match external pressure, you did not adapt. You capitulated.

You cannot articulate why you shifted. Adaptation is a choice. Choices have reasons. If you cannot explain the logic of your change, it was probably not a choice. It was a reaction.

You feel defensive about the change. Confident adaptation does not need defending. If you find yourself justifying, protecting, explaining away, something is off. The defensiveness is a signal that you are not sure you made the right move.

Others seem confused by your inconsistency. People can follow adaptation when it makes sense. When your changes confuse the people around you, it often means the changes are confusing you too. Their disorientation reflects yours.

Adaptive Presence Others Can Trust

The goal is not constant change. The goal is appropriate change. Adaptation that serves purpose. Flexibility that maintains integrity.

When you get this right, something happens in your relationships. People start to trust you more, not less. They see that your methods flex but your spine does not. They experience stability even as you respond to changing conditions. They know who you are even when they cannot predict exactly what you will do.

This is adaptive presence. Stable intent, flexible method. The people around you know your aim. They know your values. They know what you stand for. Within that frame, you have room to move. The frame is what makes the movement trustworthy.

Adaptive presence lowers tension in groups. When people trust that your core is stable, they relax about the surface variations. They do not have to monitor you for sudden changes in direction. They do not have to protect themselves against your unpredictability. The trust you build through consistent purpose gives you more freedom to adapt your approach.

The line between flexibility and unreliability is purpose. Flexibility in service of purpose is adaptive. Movement without purpose is just chaos.

The Test

Adaptability proves itself in practice.

When conditions change, do you respond from center or react from pressure? When the room shifts, do you adjust your tactics or abandon your aim? When people push back, do you hold what matters and flex what can move, or do you either break or collapse?

These are the questions that test adaptability.

The sovereign man is not rigid. He does not insist on one way because one way is all he knows. He has range. He can move.

The sovereign man is not compliant. He does not become whatever the room wants because avoiding friction is easier than holding his ground. He has a spine. He can hold.

He reads conditions. He assesses what serves his purpose. He chooses his approach. And he remains, through every adaptation, the same man at center. Governed from inside. Directing himself. Sovereign.

The Art of Adaptability:
Hold Your Course, Adjust Your Sails

THE ADAPTIVE
(Sovereign)

THE REACTIVE
(Rigid or Compliant)

Adjusts their approach while maintaining their core purpose. They have a rudder and use it.

Either breaks from being too rigid or drifts by complying with every external pressure.

THE TEST: PURPOSE IS THE COMPASS
Ask yourself: Does this change serve my ultimate goal, or does it abandon it to avoid discomfort?

THE FOUNDATION: A STABLE CENTER

Like a martial artist, a stable internal core is what makes flexible, powerful movement possible.

WARNING SIGN: DEFENSIVENESS

If you feel the need to justify or defend a change, you have likely reacted, not adapted.

Chapter 8

The Authority

You do not arrive at this book with a clean slate.

You arrive with weight. Some of it comes from the assault itself. The pressures that squeezed you into patterns you did not choose. But some of it comes from what happened while you were under assault. Somewhere along the way, you handed over authority. Not in one dramatic moment. In a hundred small ones. Each handoff felt like practicality, or peace-keeping, or just getting through the day. None of them felt like surrender.

But that is what they were.

This chapter is about seeing where authority went. Not to assign blame. Not to wallow. To see clearly, because seeing is the first act of taking it back.

The Quiet Handoff

Authority does not leave with an announcement. It leaves in the spaces between words. In the things you stopped saying. In the decisions that started happening around you instead of through you.

The conversation you stopped having.

There was a topic. Something that mattered. Maybe it was how money got spent. Maybe it was how the kids were being raised. Maybe it was something in the marriage that had gone cold. You brought it up once. Or twice. It went badly. The response was defensive, or dismissive, or turned into a fight that solved nothing.

So you stopped. Not officially. You just let the topic drop. Weeks passed. Then months. The issue did not resolve. It just became one of those things you work around. You told yourself you were picking your battles. What you were doing was ceding territory.

That territory did not come back. The pattern set. She decides that. You do not bring it up. The boundary of your authority quietly moved inward, and you helped move it.

The decision that happened without you.

You came home and something had changed. A purchase was made. A commitment was scheduled. A choice about the kids was finalized. You were informed, not consulted. Your input was not requested because your input had stopped mattering.

This did not happen overnight. It happened because you were not present when the smaller decisions were being made. You were working. You were checked out. You were in the room but not in the conversation. Presence is a vote. Absence is a forfeit. Enough forfeits and they stop calling the vote.

Now the pattern is set. Things happen. You find out later. You have opinions, but the opinions come too late to matter. You have been demoted from partner to informed party. The demotion happened quietly, and part of you was relieved because it meant less to carry. But something in you knows what you traded.

The body you stopped governing.

There was a time you decided what you ate, when you moved, how you treated your own flesh. That time faded. Now the schedule decides. The stress decides. The path of least resistance decides.

You eat what is fast. You skip the workout because the day was long. You pour the drink because the evening needs something. You stay up too late because the quiet hours are the only ones that feel like yours. Each choice makes sense in isolation. Exposed as a pattern, they reveal a man who has handed governance of his own body to circumstance.

The body keeps score. It does not argue with you. It simply reflects what has been chosen. The weight. The stiffness. The fatigue that sleep does not fix. These are not failures of discipline. They are evidence of who has been in charge. And it has not been you.

The inner life you abandoned.

There was a time you knew what you felt. Wanted things. Dreamed about things. Had preferences that were yours alone.

That interior space got crowded out. The demands were loud. The feelings were inconvenient. So you muted them. You focused on function. You handled what needed handling and stopped asking what you actually wanted.

Now when someone asks what you want, there is a pause. The question feels strange. You have become so fluent in what is needed, what is expected, what keeps the peace, that your own desires went underground. They surface sometimes. A flash of longing. A moment of rage that seems disproportionate to the trigger. These are signals from a self you stopped consulting.

You did not abandon yourself dramatically. You just stopped checking in. And after enough silence, the voice inside got quieter.

The friendships you let die.

You used to have friends. Not acquaintances. Friends. Men who knew you. Men you could call.

You do not know exactly when it stopped. The busyness was real. The obligations multiplied. Reaching out felt like one more thing on a list that was already too long. So you let the connections thin. You told yourself they understood. Everyone was busy. It was just life.

Now you look up and the friendships are gone. Or they are hollow. Men you see occasionally and talk to about nothing. The loneliness is real but hard to name because you are surrounded by people. None of them know you. That is not their failure. You stopped letting them in. You stopped showing up. The absence compounded.

A man without friends is a man without witnesses. No one sees him clearly. No one calls him on his drift. No one knows when he is off center because no one has seen him centered. This isolation did not happen to you. You let it happen. You chose convenience over connection enough times that the connections dissolved.

The standards you quietly lowered.

You used to have lines. Things you would not accept. Ways you expected to be treated. Levels of effort you demanded from yourself.

Those lines moved. Not all at once. In increments. You accepted something you said you would not accept because fighting it was exhausting. You let a standard slide because holding it felt like too much. You told yourself you were being flexible. Mature. Realistic.

Maybe you were. Or maybe you were training everyone around you, including yourself, that your lines were negotiable. That your word did not hold. That your standards were suggestions, not commitments.

A man whose lines keep moving is a man who cannot be relied upon. Others learn this. They push and the line moves. They push again. It moves again. Eventually they stop asking where the line is because they know it will move to wherever is convenient.

You did this to yourself. Not because you are weak. Because you were tired, and moving the line was easier than holding it. The cost came later.

How You Know

The handoffs leave marks. They show up in the body, in the mind, in the emotional field. Most men have normalized these signals. They feel them daily and call them nothing.

They are not nothing. They are evidence.

The body tells you first.

There is a specific tension that comes from ungoverned living. It sits in the jaw, the shoulders, the lower back. It is not the tension of effort. It is the tension of bracing. The body has learned that things happen to it, not through it. So it stays tight, waiting for the next thing it will have to absorb.

You feel it when you wake up. Already braced. Before the day has asked anything of you, the body is preparing to react. This is not readiness. This is resignation wearing the mask of alertness.

There is also a heaviness. Not the heaviness of honest fatigue after good work. A heaviness that does not lift with rest. The body carrying weight it was not designed to carry because the weight was never processed. Decisions avoided. Conversations not had. Feelings not felt. The body holds all of it.

When you are governing yourself, the body feels different. Not lighter necessarily. But cleaner. Tension comes and releases. Effort depletes and rest restores. The system works because it is being worked. When you have handed over authority, the system stagnates. The tension becomes chronic. The heaviness becomes normal. You stop noticing because it is always there.

The mind shows you second.

A governed mind is clear. It knows what matters. It can distinguish between urgent and important, between signal and noise. It makes decisions and moves on.

A mind that has ceded authority is different. It spins. The same thoughts return without resolution. Decisions feel heavy because every choice might be wrong and being wrong might mean conflict. So the mind delays. Gathers more information. Waits for clarity that does not come.

This is not thoughtfulness. It is paralysis dressed as deliberation.

There is also a mental fuzziness. A difficulty focusing. Not because the mind is incapable but because the mind is not being directed. It wanders to whatever is most stimulating or most threatening. Social media. News cycles. Worst-case scenarios. The mind follows these paths because no one is steering it somewhere better.

When you are governing yourself, the mind submits to direction. You point it at a problem and it works the problem. You tell it to rest and it rests. The relationship is one of authority. When you have handed over that authority, the mind does what it wants. You become a passenger in your own head.

The emotions show you last.

Emotions are information. They tell you what matters, what is threatened, what is being violated. A man who governs himself can feel the emotion, read its message, and choose his response.

A man who has handed over authority has a different relationship with emotion. Either the emotions run the show, surging into reaction before any choice is made. Or the emotions are muted, buried so deep they barely register. Neither pattern is governance.

The reactive pattern shows up as anger that surprises you with its intensity. Small triggers producing large responses. You snap at your wife over dishes. You rage at a driver who cut you off. The anger is not about the dishes or the driver. It is about everything you have swallowed, everything you have not addressed, everything you have let slide. The anger finds an acceptable target and floods through.

The muted pattern shows up as flatness. You should feel something and you do not. Good news lands without joy. Bad news lands without grief. You move through days in a gray middle range, protected from pain but also cut off from pleasure. This is not peace. This is disconnection.

When you are governing yourself, emotions flow. They rise when they have something to say. They are felt, heard, and integrated. They do not pile up. They do not ambush. They serve their function and release.

What Taking It Back Feels Like

Recognition is not repair. Seeing where authority went does not automatically bring it back. But seeing is required. You cannot reclaim what you have not acknowledged losing.

Taking authority back is not a single act. It is not a conversation or a declaration or a dramatic moment. It is a shift in stance that shows up in ordinary moments. You feel it before anyone else sees it.

The first thing you notice is the pause.

Something happens. The old pattern starts to run. You feel the pull toward silence, or compliance, or reaction. But now there is a gap. A small space between the trigger and the response. You did not have that space before. Or you had it and never used it.

Now you use it. You feel the pull and you do not follow it automatically. You ask what is actually happening. You ask what you actually want. The pause is not long. Sometimes it is a single breath. But it is yours. You are the one who created it.

This pause is the first sign that authority is returning. The pattern no longer runs you. You are starting to run it.

Then you notice your voice coming back.

Not volume. Presence. You say something you would have swallowed before. Not because you planned to. Because it was true, and the truth came out before the old filter caught it.

It might be small. A preference stated instead of deferred. A disagreement voiced instead of buried. A question asked instead of assumed away. The words are ordinary. What is different is that you said them. You did not ask permission from the part of you that manages how others feel about you.

This is what it feels like when your voice stops waiting for approval. The words come because they are yours. The room adjusts or it does not. Either way, you spoke.

You notice choices returning to your hands.

The body. The schedule. The money. The things that had drifted into autopilot or someone else's control. You start making decisions again. Not seizing control. Just participating. Showing up before the choice is made instead of reacting after.

You eat something because you chose it, not because it was there. You move because you decided to, not because you found a window. You say yes or no based on what actually works, not based on what avoids friction.

Each choice is small. But the accumulation matters. You are learning that your preferences count. That your participation is expected. That you have a vote and you are casting it.

You notice the body starting to trust you again.

The chronic tension does not vanish overnight. But something shifts. The bracing loosens in moments when you realize you are governing. The jaw unclenches. The shoulders drop. The breath moves lower.

This happens because the body is getting evidence. It is being consulted. It is being moved with intention instead of dragged through reaction. Bodies learn from experience. When you govern, the body registers safety. When you drift, it registers threat. It has been registering threat for a long time. Now it is getting different data.

The shift is not dramatic. It is a slow thaw. You feel it in moments. A morning when you wake up and the brace is not already locked in. An evening when the heaviness lifts without alcohol. These moments are evidence. They tell you the body is starting to believe what you are showing it.

You notice that the inner voice has something to say.

You asked it a question. What do you want? At first there was silence. Or confusion. The question was too unfamiliar.

Now there is an answer. Faint at first. A flicker of preference. A pull toward something. A quiet no that is actually a no, not just a reaction to pressure.

This voice was never gone. It was buried. Muted by years of responding to what was expected instead of what was wanted. The voice comes back when it is consulted. When it learns that its answers matter. When it realizes you are listening again.

You do not have to act on everything it says. Sometimes the want conflicts with reality. But you hear it. You let it register. You stop treating your own desires as inconvenient noise.

You notice that holding a line feels different.

There is a moment when the push comes. Someone wants you to move the line. The old pattern would have calculated cost and benefit, would have found a reason to flex, would have told itself that this was not the hill.

Now the line does not move. Not with anger. Not with drama. It just stays where you put it. The push meets something solid.

This is not rigidity. Rigid men break. This is something else. You know where the line is because you put it there on purpose. You know why it matters. When the push comes, you do not have to decide in the moment whether to hold. The decision was already made. The line is the line.

What surprises you is how little energy it takes. Holding the line is not a fight. It is a fact. You stand there. The line stays. The world adjusts.

You notice you are the same person in different rooms.

Work. Home. Friends. The mask changes used to be automatic. Different posture. Different voice. Different version of you calibrated to what each room expected.

Now the calibration feels less necessary. You show up and you are who you are. The tone adjusts because different rooms need different tones. But the center does not shift. The spine stays the same.

This is what it feels like when you stop auditioning. When your presence is not a performance shaped by the audience. When you trust that who you are is enough for the room, and if it is not, that is information, not a verdict.

The Return Is the Work

There is no moment when authority fully returns. No day when the work is done. You will drift. The old patterns are deep.

Pressure will push you toward them. You will hand over authority again without noticing.

This is not failure. This is the terrain.

The practice is noticing the drift and returning to center. The practice is seeing where authority slipped and taking it back. Not perfectly. Not permanently. But repeatedly. For as long as you live.

The man who practices this is not better than other men. He is not stronger or smarter or more disciplined. He has simply seen where his authority went. He has felt what it costs to live without it. And he has decided, again and again, to take it back.

The next chapter makes that decision visible.

The Quiet Surrender: Where Your Authority Went

Authority is not lost in one dramatic moment, but surrendered in a hundred small handoffs that feel like practicality or peace-keeping.

THE CONVERSATION YOU STOPPED HAVING

To avoid conflict, you stopped raising important topics, quietly ceding that territory.

THE DECISION THAT HAPPENED WITHOUT YOU

Your absence from small choices led to you being informed about big ones, not consulted.

THE FRIENDSHIPS YOU LET DIE

You chose convenience over connection, letting friendships thin until you were isolated.

THE STANDARDS YOU QUIETLY LOWERED

To avoid exhaustion, you moved your own lines, teaching others your standards were negotiable.

THE INNER LIFE YOU ABANDONED

You stopped checking in with what you truly wanted, becoming fluent only in what was expected.

Chapter 9

The Sovereign State

The Core of It

Sovereignty means governing yourself.

Not being governed by the expectations others have of you. Not being governed by the scripts your father handed down. Not being governed by the fear of what people might think, the hunger for validation, or the pain you are trying to avoid.

Governing yourself. From the inside out.

This is the central claim of everything you have read. A man can learn to govern his own state. He can choose his response rather than having it chosen for him by conditioning, circumstance, or pressure. He can become the one who directs his life rather than the one who reacts to it.

The word for being governed by external forces is external reactive. Something happens, and you respond from pattern. The stimulus controls the response. You are moved.

The word for governing yourself is internal directed. Something happens, and you choose your response based on your aim. Your purpose controls the response. You move.

The difference between these two modes is the difference between a life that happens to you and a life you build. Between being shaped by every pressure and shaping yourself despite them. Between drifting through your days and directing them.

Middle-aged men face particular pressure to become external reactive. The assault is real. The roles multiply. The expectations compound. The old maps fail. Under that pressure, most men slide into one of three reactive paths: gripping harder, performing emptily, or withdrawing entirely. Each path feels like a solution. Each path is actually surrender. Each path hands governance to forces outside the self.

The Sovereign State is the refusal of that surrender. It is the commitment to govern yourself even when the pressure mounts. Especially when the pressure mounts.

This does not mean perfection. You will still react. You will still drift. You will still have days when the old patterns run the show. Sovereignty is not a permanent achievement. It is a practice. The practice of noticing when you have handed over governance and taking it back. The practice of returning to center, again and again, for as long as you live.

The man who practices this is not better than other men. He is simply freer. Free to choose his response. Free to act from purpose. Free to be the same man in every room because he is governed from the same center in every room.

That freedom is what this book has been about. Everything else is structure to support it.

What This Book Has Shown

The assault is real, but the paths men take in response make it worse.

Red Pill grips harder and burns relationships. Hollow State performs and empties out. The Void withdraws and disappears. Each path is external reactive. Each path hands governance to forces outside the self. Each path makes the problem worse while pretending to solve it.

Center is the foundation of self-governance.

Center is not a destination. It is a cultivated state where your nervous system has settled enough that you can see clearly, interrogate your reactions, and choose your response. Center is the commitment to self-governance made physical. Without center, you have intention but no capacity. With center, you have the ground to stand on.

Purpose prevents drift.

Without purpose, every stimulus looks urgent. With purpose, you can sort what matters from what does not. Long purpose is your due north. Immediate purpose is what this moment requires. The question "what serves my aim?" is not productivity advice. It is how you stay internal directed when pressure tries to take over.

Adaptability is not surrender.

Rigidity breaks. Compliance drifts. True adaptability holds the aim and shifts the method. Your values stay fixed. Your tactics move with conditions. This is strength that bends without breaking. This is governance that responds to reality without being governed by it.

The shift is measurable.

External reactive to internal directed. That is the change you are making. You will still oscillate. Everyone does. The goal is not perfection. The goal is reducing the frequency of drift and increasing the time spent governing from inside. Track the ratio. Watch it shift.

For Reflection

Am I choosing from center, or following a script?

The old scripts are external. They tell you what a man should do based on someone else's definition. The Sovereign State does not replace one script with another. It builds the capacity to choose in the moment, from your own center, based on what the situation actually requires.

Have I asked before I acted?

What is real here? What serves my aim? These questions interrupt the automatic sequence. They create the pause where governance becomes possible. The questions are the practice.

Am I adapting without breaking?

Conditions change. You change with them. But you do not lose your spine in the process. You know what stays fixed and what can move. You adjust tactics without abandoning values.

Am I the same man in every room?

Not the same behavior. The same center. The voice changes. The spine does not. People meet the same governing center whether they find me at work, at home, or in the world.

The Life That Becomes Possible

Knowing the framework is not the same as living it. But living it changes things.

The man who practices this wakes up differently. Not with dread. Not with the weight of performance already pressing down. He wakes up with orientation. He knows what he stands for. He knows what he is building. The day ahead is terrain to move through, not a gauntlet to survive.

He walks into rooms differently. Not scanning for threats. Not calculating how to be seen. Present. Grounded. Available for whatever the room actually needs. People feel this. They may not name it, but they relax in his presence. They trust him before they know why.

He handles pressure differently. The old triggers still fire. The patterns still try to run. But there is space now. A pause that was not there before. In that pause, he can see what is happening. He can choose. The reaction does not own him the way it used to.

He fails differently. The miss still stings. The drift still happens. But he does not collapse into shame or harden into defense. He sees it. He owns it. He repairs what he can. He returns to center and continues. The failure becomes data, not verdict.

He loves differently. Not performing. Not withdrawing. Not gripping. Present. The people closest to him start to trust that he will be there. Not perfect, but there. The same man today that he was yesterday. The same man he will be tomorrow.

He ages differently. The losses still come. The body still changes. The roles still shift. But he is not anchored to what is disappearing. He is anchored to what remains. The center holds even when the circumstances do not.

This is not a fantasy. It is what becomes possible when a man commits to governing himself. Not perfectly. Not permanently. But more often than not. More consistently than before.

The practice is simple. Return to center. Ask what is real. Ask what serves. Choose your response. When you drift, return again.

The results compound. The ratio shifts. The man who started reactive becomes the man who is mostly governed from inside. The people around him notice. The life he is building takes shape.

This is available to you. Not because you are special. Because you are willing to practice.

Reactive vs. Directed: Choose Your State

EXTERNAL REACTIVE:
A Life That Happens To You

Governed by the Outside
Stimulus controls the response. You are moved by pressure, fear, and expectations.

Common Paths are Traps

Gripping harder   Performing emptily

Withdrawing

INTERNAL DIRECTED:
A Life You Build

Governed from Within
Your purpose controls the response. You choose your actions based on your aim.

The Practice of Freedom

Return to center   Ask what serves your aim

Choose your response

These actions are all forms of surrendering control

Glossary

Adaptability - The capacity to adjust tactics while holding aim. Not compromise, not surrender. Staying internal directed while responding to real conditions. Your values stay fixed. Your methods move with circumstances.

The Assault - The convergence of pressures facing middle-aged men: role confusion, cultural hostility, physical decline, professional plateau, relational strain. The assault is real. The three paths are failed responses to it.

Body Levers - The physical tools for regulating your nervous system: breath (long exhale), posture (grounded, shoulders down), tension release (scan and let go), and grounding (felt contact with present moment). The body is the fastest lever because your nervous system listens to your body before your thoughts.

Center - The aligned state of body, mind, and emotion that lets a man choose instead of react. Center is where self-rule becomes possible. When these three align, you can pause, feel the ground, and choose your next step without panic. Center is a practice, not a destination.

Centering - A two-part act: psychological intent ("Back to center") plus biological regulation (breath, posture, tension release, grounding). The intent directs. The body executes. Centering is how you return to center when you have drifted.

The Compact - The agreement with yourself that defines sovereign living: I choose from center, not from script. I ask before I act. I adapt without breaking. I repair without defense. I stay the same man in every room.

External Reactive - A mode of being where behavior, attention, and emotional state are primarily shaped by stimuli outside the self. Primary driver: what happens to you. Decision pattern: respond first, interpret later. Emotional signature: volatility. You are governed, not governing. The three paths (Red Pill, Hollow State, Void) are all forms of external reactive living locked in place.

The Eye - Centered seeing. The capacity for calm observation available when you are grounded. From center, the Eye asks two questions before every move: What is real here? What serves the aim? The Eye is not passive watching. It is active judgment that prepares decisive action.

The Four Principles - The pillars that hold the Sovereign State steady: presence, intent, adaptation, and integration. Each speaks to a habit of mind and body that shapes every choice. Missing any pillar weakens the others.

Grounding - The felt sense of contact with the present moment through the body. Feeling your feet on the floor, your weight in the chair, your hands where they rest. Grounding pulls you into the moment you can actually govern.

Hollow State - One of the three failed paths. External reactive to expectation. The man performs competence while feeling empty inside. He meets every demand, checks every box, but has lost connection to why any of it matters. He is governed by what others expect of him.

The Hub - The center of the wheel from which all spokes (roles) extend. A man governed from the hub is stable across roles. Pressure on one spoke does not collapse the others. The hub is center applied to the structure of your life.

Immediate Purpose - What this moment requires from the man you are choosing to be. The aim in this room, this conversation, this day. Immediate purpose changes constantly and should align with long purpose.

Integration - One of the four principles. Pulling strength, empathy, and reason into one current. Strength provides courage to act. Empathy reads context. Reason checks facts. When these forces align, decisions flow. Also: being the same man across all your roles. The voice changes. The spine does not.

Intent - One of the four principles. The answer to "Why am I about to move?" Intent cuts away noise and aligns choices with deeper values rather than quick emotion. When intent leads, time and talent stop leaking into tasks that do not fit your aim.

Internal Directed - A mode of being where behavior, attention, and emotional state are guided by an internally chosen aim and center, regardless of external conditions. Primary driver: what you intend. Decision pattern: orient first, then act. Emotional signature: stability. You govern yourself.

Long Purpose - Your overarching direction in life. What you stand for. What you build toward. Who you serve beyond yourself. Long purpose does not change often. It is the foundation that immediate purposes connect to.

Meta-loss - The slow erosion of identity that happens when external markers (roles, titles, status, physical capacity) disappear and nothing internal remains to anchor you. Meta-loss drives men toward the three failed paths. It is what happens when a man has built his identity on things that can be taken away.

Neuroception - The body's unconscious scanning for safety or threat. Your nervous system reads the environment and adjusts your state before your conscious mind gets involved.

Understanding neuroception explains why the body must be addressed first.

Oscillation - The movement between external reactive and internal directed modes. All men oscillate. The objective is not eliminating oscillation but reducing its frequency and increasing time spent internal directed. Track the ratio. Watch it shift.

The Pause - The space between stimulus and response. This is where sovereignty exists. External reactive collapses the pause. Internal directed expands it. Building the pause is a skill developed through practice.

Presence - One of the four principles. Noticing what is happening inside and around you without judgment. Clear perception in real time. A man who lacks presence walks through rooms but misses signals.

Purpose Over Perfection - The operating principle that frees action. Perfection is a finish line that shifts each time you draw near. Purpose is a compass that keeps pointing even when the trail twists. Purpose lets you step, check, and adjust because the aim is direction, not flawlessness.

Red Pill - One of the three failed paths. External reactive to perceived threats to status. The man grips harder, asserts dominance, views relationships as power contests. He burns connections while believing he is finally seeing clearly. He is governed by his fear of losing status.

The Return - The practice of coming back to center after drifting. Not punishment for having drifted, simply what you do. Every return is a rep that builds capacity. The return, not the drift, defines the sovereign man.

The Sovereign State - The framework for self-governance presented in this book. Not a destination but a practice. The ongoing commitment to govern yourself from the inside out rather than being governed by external forces. The refusal to surrender to the three reactive paths.

Sovereignty - Governing yourself. Choosing your response rather than having it chosen for you by conditioning, circumstance, or pressure. The capacity to be internal directed even when external forces push toward reactivity.

The Storm - Centered force. The capacity for decisive action available when you are grounded. The Storm uses power in service of clear intent. It comes from the core, hits the target, and then settles again. Centered force is sized force, matching what the moment actually needs.

The Three Paths - Red Pill, Hollow State, and Void. The three common responses to the assault on middle-aged masculinity. Each feels like a solution but is actually surrender. Each is a form of external reactive living locked in place.

The Triangle - Body, mind, and emotion working as one system. When these three corners align, that alignment is center. Physical stability enables mental clarity. Mental clarity helps you understand your emotions. Emotional awareness tells you what matters. When all three align around purpose, you move as a whole person.

Trigger Audit - The practice of examining your reactive patterns. Something happens. You get triggered. You react. The audit asks: Where did that come from? Does it serve my purpose? If not, what would? Applies to negative and positive triggers equally.

Void - One of the three failed paths. External reactive to criticism or the possibility of failure. The man withdraws, makes himself smaller, disengages from life to avoid being hurt or judged. He is governed by his fear of exposure.

"What is real here?" - The first governance question. Understanding the full landscape of the moment: what is actually happening externally, how you are feeling, how you are reacting, what pattern is trying to fire. You cannot govern what you cannot see.

"What serves my aim?" - The second governance question. The pivot between external reactive and internal directed. Asks whether your proposed response comes from purpose or from conditioning. Forces the choice into the open.

Window of Tolerance - The zone where your nervous system is regulated enough that you can think clearly and choose deliberately. Outside this window (too activated or too shut down), governance becomes difficult or impossible. The body levers help you return to this window.

Appendix

A. The Sovereign State Overview

The Core Claim

Sovereignty means governing yourself. Not being governed by expectations, scripts, fear of judgment, or the hunger for validation. Governing yourself from the inside out.

The Sovereign State is not a destination. It is a practice. The ongoing commitment to choose your response rather than have it chosen for you by conditioning, circumstance, or pressure.

The Behavioral Objective

The framework exists to produce one measurable shift: moving from external reactive to internal directed.

External reactive means your behavior, attention, and emotional state are shaped by stimuli outside yourself. Something happens and you respond from pattern. You are governed.

Internal directed means your behavior, attention, and emotional state are guided by an internally chosen aim and center. Something happens and you choose your response based on purpose. You govern.

The goal is not perfection. It is reducing how often you get knocked into reactive mode and increasing the time spent internally directed.

The Foundation: Center

Center is the aligned state of body, mind, and emotion that makes self-rule possible.

When these three align, you can pause, see clearly, and choose your response without panic. Without center, sovereignty is just a word. You react, perform, or hide. From center, you can actually govern.

Center is not a mood or a feeling. It is a condition of the system. The body settles. The mind clears. Emotion fits the moment. Something clicks into place.

The Triangle

Body, mind, and emotion form the three corners of a triangle. When all three align, that alignment is center.

Body - Settled and ready. Weight grounded. Muscles available, not braced. Breath low and slow.

Mind - One clear signal instead of competing noise. The aim is visible. Focus without strain.

Emotion - Contact without flooding. Feeling present but not running the show. Emotion fits the situation and fuels action instead of hijacking it.

When the corners conflict, governance fails. When they align, you move as a whole person.

The Two Capacities: Eye and Storm

From center, two capacities become available. These are not tools you pick up. They are what seeing and acting look like when you are grounded.

The Eye is centered seeing. Calm observation from steady footing. Before every move, it asks: What is real here? What serves my aim?

The Storm is centered force. Decisive action in service of clear intent. It comes from the core, hits the target, and settles again. Sized force that matches what the moment actually needs.

A man knocked off center has access to neither. His calm is numbness. His force is reactive. From center, both become clean.

The Four Principles

Four pillars hold the Sovereign State steady.

Presence - Noticing what is happening inside and around you without judgment. Clear perception in real time.

Intent - The answer to "Why am I about to move?" Aligning choices with deeper values rather than quick emotion.

Adaptation - Readiness to bend without cracking. Holding core values while adjusting tactics to match real conditions.

Integration - Pulling strength, empathy, and reason into one current. Being the same man across all roles. The voice changes. The spine does not.

Purpose: The Direction

Purpose prevents drift. Without it, every stimulus looks urgent. With it, you can sort what matters from what does not.

Long purpose is your overarching direction. What you stand for. What you build toward. Who you serve beyond yourself.

Immediate purpose is what this moment requires. The aim in this room, this conversation, this day.

When the two align, your small moves add up to something.

Purpose Over Perfection

Perfection is a finish line that shifts each time you draw near. Purpose is a compass that keeps pointing even when the trail twists.

Perfection freezes. Purpose frees. You step, check, and adjust because the aim is direction, not flawlessness.

The Three Failed Paths

Under pressure, men reach for something. Three common responses look like solutions but end in surrender.

Red Pill - External reactive to status threats. The man grips harder, asserts dominance, views relationships as power contests. He is governed by the scoreboard.

Hollow State - External reactive to expectations. The man performs competence while feeling empty inside. He meets every demand but has lost connection to why any of it matters. He is governed by the role.

Void - External reactive to criticism. The man withdraws, makes himself smaller, disengages to avoid being hurt or judged. He is governed by the critics.

Each path hands control to something outside the self. Each is a form of external reactive living locked in place.

The Two Governance Questions

These questions interrupt the automatic sequence. They create the pause where choice becomes possible.

What is real here? - Understanding the full landscape of the moment. What is actually happening. How you are feeling. What pattern is trying to fire.

What serves my aim? - The pivot between reactive and directed. Asking whether your proposed response comes from purpose or from conditioning.

The Pause and The Return

The Pause is the space between stimulus and response. This is where sovereignty exists. External reactive collapses it. Internal directed expands it.

The Return is the practice of coming back to center after drifting. Not punishment for having drifted. Simply what you do. Every return builds capacity. The return, not the drift, defines the sovereign man.

The Summary

Sovereignty is self-governance. Center is the foundation. Eye and Storm are the capacities. Purpose is the direction. The Triangle keeps body, mind, and emotion aligned. The four principles hold the structure steady. The two questions interrupt reaction and create choice.

External reactive to internal directed. That is the shift. That is the work.

B. Centering Body Regulation Tools

These are practical techniques for settling your nervous system. They work because your body signals safety or threat to your brain. Change what the body is doing, and the system follows.

Use these tools to return to center, to widen the pause, or to recover after activation. None require equipment, privacy, or explanation. You can use them in a meeting, in your car, in the middle of a conversation.

Extended Exhale

The simplest tool. Works anywhere.

A long exhale activates the calming branch of your nervous system. When exhale is longer than inhale, your body reads safety.

The practice: Inhale normally through your nose. Exhale slowly through your mouth, letting it be longer than your inhale. Empty the lungs fully. Let the next inhale come naturally. Repeat 3-5 times.

No counting required. Just make the exhale slow and complete. Three breaths can shift your state. Ten can shift it significantly.

Box Breathing

More structured. Useful when you need focus.

The practice: Inhale for 4 counts. Hold for 4 counts. Exhale for 4 counts. Hold for 4 counts. Repeat 4-6 cycles.

The holds are what make this different from normal breathing. They require attention, which pulls you out of spiraling thoughts.

The rhythm is calming. The structure gives your mind something to do.

If 4 counts feels too long, use 3. If it feels too short, use 5. The ratio matters more than the specific count.

Physiological Sigh

Fast reset. One or two breaths can work.

This is a natural pattern your body uses during sleep and crying. Doing it deliberately triggers the same calming effect.

The practice: Inhale through your nose. At the top of the inhale, take a second short inhale (a "sip" of air). Exhale slowly and fully through your mouth.

The double inhale reinflates collapsed air sacs in your lungs. The long exhale activates the calming response. One or two of these can shift your state faster than multiple normal breaths.

Tension Release Sequence

Your body stores activation as tension. This sequence releases it.

The practice:

Jaw: Notice if your teeth are clenched or pressed together. Let your jaw hang slightly open. Let the tongue rest on the floor of your mouth.

Shoulders: Notice if your shoulders are raised toward your ears. Drop them. Let them fall away from your neck.

Hands: Notice if your fists are clenched or your fingers are tight. Open your hands. Let them rest with fingers loose.

Gut: Notice if your stomach is tight or braced. Let it soften. Let your breath reach your belly.

You can run through all four in 30 seconds. Do it at your desk, in traffic, before a difficult conversation. Each release tells your system the threat has passed.

Grounding

Pulls you into the present moment through physical sensation.

The practice:

Feet: Feel your feet on the floor. Notice the pressure, the weight, the contact. Press down slightly and feel the floor press back.

Weight: Feel your body's weight in the chair or where you stand. Let gravity hold you. Stop bracing against it.

Hands: Feel your hands where they rest. The temperature. The texture of what they touch.

This works because anxiety lives in the future and regret lives in the past. Your body is always in the present. Grounding uses that fact. You cannot govern yesterday or tomorrow. You can only govern now. Grounding puts you in the moment you can actually govern.

Movement Release

Sometimes stillness is not enough. The body needs to complete the stress cycle through motion.

Options: Walk, even for 5 minutes. Shake out your hands vigorously for 30 seconds. Roll your shoulders, forward and back.

Stretch your neck slowly side to side. Push against a wall or doorframe and release.

The point is not exercise. The point is letting the body discharge what it is holding. After activation, your system may have mobilized energy that has nowhere to go. Movement gives it somewhere to go.

Choosing the Right Tool

For quick reset in the moment: Physiological sigh (1-2 breaths)

For general calming: Extended exhale (3-10 breaths)

For focus and structure: Box breathing (4-6 cycles)

For releasing held tension: Tension release sequence

For pulling out of spiraling thoughts: Grounding

For after significant activation: Movement release

You will learn what works for your system. Experiment. Notice what actually shifts your state. Build your own toolkit from what works.

C. Path Reflection

The three failed paths described in Chapter 2 are not personality types. They are response patterns. Under pressure, most men drift toward one more than the others. Some men shift between two depending on context. A few cycle through all three.

This reflection helps you notice which pull is strongest for you. The goal is not a label. The goal is recognition. When you see the pattern starting to run, you have a chance to catch it before it completes.

Red Pill Pattern

This path grips harder. It reads threat in every interaction and responds with control, dominance, or competition. The man on this path hands governance to the scoreboard. His worth rises and falls with status.

Recognition markers:

You might lean toward this pattern if:

- Criticism lands as attack. Your first response is to counter, not consider.
- You scan rooms for who respects you and who does not.
- Conversations become competitions you need to win.
- Backing down feels like losing, even when the stakes are low.
- You interrupt, explain, or correct more than you listen.
- Apologies feel like surrender.
- Rest feels like falling behind.
- You measure days by what you dominated, not what you built.

Key questions:

When someone disagrees with you, what happens in your body? Do you feel heat, tension, the pull to push back before you have fully heard them?

How important is respect to you? Not as a value, but as a need. Does a day without visible respect feel like a day you lost?

When you are honest with yourself, how many of your actions are about winning versus how many are about building?

The pull:

This path promises safety through strength. If you are dominant enough, no one can hurt you. If you win enough, your worth is beyond question. The pull is strong because the world does reward strength. The trap is that the scoreboard never stops. There is always another challenge, another threat, another person who does not show proper respect. Governance stays outside. You react to every provocation because every provocation threatens the position you are defending.

Hollow State Pattern

This path performs. It meets every demand, checks every box, and feels nothing inside. The man on this path hands governance to the role. He becomes what is expected and loses contact with what he wants.

Recognition markers:

You might lean toward this pattern if:

- You handle everything and feel nothing.
- People call you reliable, solid, dependable. You feel empty.

- You cannot remember the last time you felt genuinely excited about something.
- When asked what you want, your mind goes blank or jumps to what you should want.
- You have trouble identifying emotions in your body. You know you are stressed because of circumstances, not because you feel it.
- Weekends feel like recovery, not life.
- You go through motions that used to mean something.
- You are tired in a way that sleep does not fix.

Key questions:

When did you last feel fully alive? Not functioning, not handling it, but actually present and engaged? How long ago was that?

If every obligation disappeared tomorrow, what would you do? If the answer does not come quickly, that is information.

Do you know what you feel right now, in your body? Not what you think, but what you feel? Can you name it?

The pull:

This path promises safety through performance. If you meet every expectation, no one can fault you. If you handle everything, you have value. The pull is strong because the world does reward reliability. The trap is that the performance becomes the person. You keep producing, but the one who would enjoy the results has checked out. Governance stays outside. The role dictates, and you execute. What you actually want stops being a question you ask.

Void Pattern

This path withdraws. It makes the self smaller to avoid judgment, conflict, or failure. The man on this path hands governance to the critics. He disappears rather than risk being seen and found lacking.

Recognition markers:

You might lean toward this pattern if:

- You avoid situations where you might be judged or evaluated.
- Your opinions soften or vanish when others push back.
- You say "I don't care" or "whatever you think" more than you say what you actually want.
- Conflict feels dangerous. You will give ground to avoid it.
- You have stopped trying things because you might fail at them.
- You feel invisible, and part of you prefers it that way.
- Energy is low. Getting through the day is the goal.
- You have trouble remembering what you used to care about.

Key questions:

When did you last take a clear position and hold it when someone disagreed? Not fight about it, just hold it. How did that feel?

What are you avoiding? Not avoiding because it is unimportant, but avoiding because it matters and you are afraid to fail at it?

If no one could judge you, what would you do differently? The gap between that answer and your current life is the territory the Void has claimed.

The pull:

This path promises safety through absence. If you do not try, you cannot fail. If you have no position, no one can attack it. If you disappear, you cannot be hurt. The pull is strong because judgment does hurt, and failure does sting. The trap is that the safety is empty. You avoid pain by avoiding life. Governance stays outside. The critics you imagine hold more power than any real person because they live in your head and never stop watching.

Mixed Patterns

Most men do not fit cleanly into one path. You might grip at work and withdraw at home. You might perform for your family and compete with your peers. You might cycle through all three depending on the pressure.

This is normal. The patterns are responses to pressure, not fixed traits. Different pressures pull toward different paths.

What matters is noticing which pull is active right now. When you feel the drift starting, you can name it. That is where the catch happens. That is where you choose to return to center instead of completing the pattern.

What to Do With This

This reflection is not a diagnosis. It is a mirror.

If you recognize yourself in one of these patterns, you now have a name for something that was running without a name. Those alone change things. Patterns that run unnamed run unchecked. Patterns you can see, you can interrupt.

The next time you feel the pull, notice it. Name which path is pulling. Then use what you have learned: settle the body, ask the questions, choose your response.

The pattern is not you. It is something you do under pressure. You can do something else.

D. Trigger Audit

The trigger audit is a practice for examining your reactive patterns. Use it after you notice a reaction, or when you see the same pattern repeating.

The goal is not self-criticism. The goal is understanding the machinery so you can change it.

The Questions

1. What happened?

Describe the trigger. Keep it factual. What actually occurred, separate from your interpretation?

Example: "My wife said we need to talk about the credit card bill."

2. What did I feel?

Name the emotion or body state. Anger, fear, shame, defensiveness, shutdown, urgency. Where did you feel it in your body?

Example: "Immediate tension in my chest. Felt accused. Wanted to defend myself."

3. What did I do (or want to do)?

Describe the reaction. What was the pull? What did you actually do?

Example: "I got defensive. Started explaining the charges before she even said anything was wrong."

4. Where did that come from?

This is the excavation. What old script, fear, or pattern was running? Where did you learn this response?

Example: "Money was always a fight in my parents' house. Any mention of money meant someone was about to be blamed. I learned to defend before being attacked."

5. Does this response serve my purpose?

Check the reaction against your aim. What is your purpose in this relationship, this situation? Does the reaction move you toward it or away from it?

Example: "My purpose with my wife is partnership and trust. Defending before she even said anything wrong does not serve that. It makes her feel like I am hiding something."

6. What would serve?

If the reaction does not serve, what would? What response aligns with your purpose?

Example: "Ask what she wants to discuss. Listen before responding. Stay curious, not defensive."

Using the Audit

After the fact: Run through the questions when you notice you reacted in a way that did not serve. Write it down if that helps. The act of articulating the pattern weakens its automatic grip.

In the moment: With practice, you can run a compressed version in real time. You notice the pull to react. You ask: Where is this coming from? Does it serve? What would? This takes seconds and can redirect the response before it fires.

For recurring patterns: If the same trigger keeps producing the same reaction, use the audit to go deeper. What is the underlying fear or wound? What would it take to build a different response?

Positive Triggers Count

The audit is not only for anger and fear. Positive triggers can pull you off center just as fast.

Praise. Flattery. Attraction. Status wins. A deal that lands. A compliment that inflates.

When something feels good, run the same audit. What is the pull? What would you do to get more of that feeling? Does that serve your purpose, or just the feeling?

Chasing validation is just as reactive as fleeing criticism. Both hand governance to external forces.

Sample Audit

What happened? Colleague questioned my recommendation in front of the team.

What did I feel? Heat in my face. Pulse sped up. Felt challenged, disrespected.

What did I do? Cut him off. Dismissed his point. Reasserted my position more forcefully.

Where did that come from? I learned early that showing uncertainty meant losing credibility. Any challenge to my position feels like a challenge to my competence.

Does this response serve my purpose? No. My purpose in this team is building trust and making good decisions. Shutting down questions does neither. It makes people stop bringing concerns to me.

What would serve? Pause. Ask him to say more. Consider whether his point has merit. Respond to the substance, not the feeling of being challenged.

The audit does not guarantee you will respond perfectly next time. It builds awareness. Awareness creates choice. Choice is where sovereignty lives.

About the Author

Dell Gines holds a PhD in Public Administration and has spent over two decades working in economic and community development across more than one hundred communities in the United States. That work brought him face to face with the quiet struggles of middle-aged men navigating identity, purpose, and pressure without a framework that fit.

The Sovereign State philosophy grew from that observation and from his own experience as a middle-aged man.

He writes at **www.sovereignmen.org.**

www.ingramcontent.com/pod-product-compliance
Lightning Source LLC
Chambersburg PA
CBHW071225090426
42736CB00014B/2981